A WORLD WITH A VIEW

POINTING OUT THE VIEW. *A Pastoral* (c. 1648) by Claude Lorrain.

A WORLD WITH A VIEW

An Inquiry into the Nature of Scenic Values

CHRISTOPHER TUNNARD

New Haven and London   Yale University Press   1978

Published with assistance from the foundation
established in memory of Philip Hamilton McMillan of the
Class of 1894, Yale College.

Designed by John O.C. McCrillis
and set in Electra Roman type.
Printed in the United States of America by
The Murray Printing Company, Westford, Massachusetts.

Published in Great Britain, Europe, Africa, and
Asia (except Japan) by Yale University Press,
Ltd., London. Distributed in Latin America by
Kaiman & Polon, Inc., New York City; in
Australia and New Zealand by Book & Film
Services, Artarmon, N.S.W., Australia; and in
Japan by Harper & Row, Publishers, Tokyo
Office.

Library of Congress Cataloging in Publication Data

Tunnard, Christopher.
  A world with a view.

  Includes bibliographical references and index.

  1. Landscape. 2. Nature (Aesthetics) I. Title.

BH301.L3T86 1978   111.8'5   77-13729
ISBN 0-300-02157-7

To
Christopher Russell Tunnard

molto studioso

CONTENTS

ILLUSTRATIONS

FOREWORD

It will not surprise anyone to learn that the condition of the environment has become over the last ten years a predominant concern of nations, a concern that has taken its place in the arenas of local politics and world affairs. A great leap forward has been taken, and none too soon. We can now point to rivers being cleaned up, mountains protected, and the preservation of older parts of cities which once were considered fit only for demolition. The results may be spotty and the losses still horrifying, but the public consciousness, as reflected in new laws and modes of action, has been aroused. It will not be satisfied unless the momentum continues to grow.

Something, however, has been lacking in all this activity. It has been assumed that a clean and healthy environment, in both city and country, is the proper goal to be sought, and indeed it is a basic foundation for all kinds of social betterment, to say nothing of human survival. Coupled with this aim is often found an interest in the beauties of nature (preferably "wild nature," which is fast disappearing everywhere), but this interest is more often than not centered on the preservation of endangered plant and animal life rather than on preservation of natural beauty. What is too often missing from current resolves is a recognition of basic human esthetic needs. Agriculture's losing battle with industry to retain desirable land often points this up, as does the unchecked expansion of cities into rural landscapes, or the intrusion of "high-rise" buildings or power lines on the skyline of a formerly unspoilt range of hills.

This book is concerned with that lacuna: the absence of an esthetic conscience in man's dealing with his environment. It emphasizes that care taken in future development is as important as the preservation or conservation of what exists. I have attempted to invoke what I consider to be valuable and desirable paradigms to be remembered when we undertake the multitude of choices entailed in leaving an imprint on the earth, whether it be in town or country.

In considering the city street or the river valley as "scenery," this book revives an earlier humanistic tradition which has been forgotten in the rush to admire "what's new." A long walk in the country or in some once flourishing but now forgotten neighborhood can rekindle this interest momentarily, but far more must be done. There is but a small band of landscape aficionados. It will be necessary to fix the esthetic imperative in many people's minds and to ensure that it remains at the forefront of planning with regard to the landscape. This book offers an approach which, I hope, will help strengthen and deepen the reader's understanding of the scenic values of his cultural patrimony in the modern landscape.

I wish to thank the Science Council of Japan and the International Council of Philosophy and the Humanities for invitations to give conference papers, parts of which are included here, and to the Division of Cultural Heritage, United Nations Economic, Social and Cultural Organization, for permission to use my unpublished reports as source material, as well as my articles in its publications *The Conservation of Cities* (Paris, 1975) and *The Man-Made Landscape* (1977). The Advisory Council on Historic Preservation afforded valuable information and experience during my term of office as a member, as did the invitation of the Department of Architecture of the University of New South Wales for a term in residence as Distinguished Visitor in 1968. Other sources to which I am indebted are given in the notes.

Among friends and associates who have helped in various ways are Geoffrey Baker, Helen Chillman, Elias Duek-Cohen, David Hill, Hans Blumenfeld, Bill Read, John N. Pearce, Azar Khosrovi, Hiroshi Daifuku, Harold Wise, Andrew Ritchie, John C. Pollaco, S. K. Stevens, Alexandra M. Shapiro, and Walter Creese. Of course, none of these people is responsible for the opinions expressed here. Mary Lusanna Sinclair provided expert secretarial and typing assistance.

Alan Shestack, Director, Yale University Art Gallery, and Marjorie G. Wynne, Edwin J. Beinecke Research Librarian, assisted in the search for illustrations.

Special thanks are due Judy Metro, Lynn Walterick, and John McCrillis of the Yale University Press for editing and layout.

Christopher Tunnard

PROLEGOMENA: LANDSCAPE WITH FIGURES

We are all familiar with that part of the landscape painter's stock-in-trade, a foreground peopled with figures, singly or in groups, one of them pointing out the view as if to guide us, the spectators, as well as his imaginary companions . . . "someone who motions with his hand to look," as the great humanist Alberti said. In our turn we explore the painted distances, from the old cottage by the side of the road or the ruined temple by the shore to the gleam of water in the distance and the sunset clouds above the horizon. Whether the painting is by Canaletto, Claude, or Constable, we usually find the figures in their various aspects of repose or animation serving as minor but necessary elements in the composition.

These are the landscapes we all know and can relate to our own experience of outdoor views and prospects. Man as a necessary but congenial part of the landscape scene, embarking for Cythera, enjoying a picnic, or, more prosaically, ploughing a furrow or reaping the grain. Our view of the landscape is conditioned by familiarity.

Lately, however—or, to be precise, for the past hundred years, but vastly accelerated today—more sinister groups and intrusions can be found in familiar landscapes. Men in work clothes are carving huge gouges out of mountainsides with modern earth-moving equipment, great bodies of water are flooding narrow valleys, high tension wires are marching over hill and dale. Megaports for oil tankers are changing the coastlines of the world—all planned by men with charts and blueprints in their hands. Helicopters are clacking over the fields, trucks are roaring through the city streets, cranes are piling vast quantities of waste on barges which dump it out at sea: the landscape, the ocean around us, and the air above us are filled with mechanical operations obeying the laws of applied technology. Nowadays the business-suited figures who might point the way are hidden on the upper floors of a city skyscraper; if they look out the window at a view it is a rare occurrence. They are too busy, and the nearest they get to nature is for a weekend round of golf.

1

Lessons are to be had from an earlier time. The landscape is a storehouse of impressions, of knowledge, of loyalty. "Whenever I am far from home," says Camillus, whom Livy called the second founder of Rome, "if I think of my country, these are the sights that rise before my eyes . . . these fields, this Tiber, the countryside I know so well, and the sky under which I was born and grew up." The landscape and the town remain, in spite of all that besets them, a source of inspiration acknowledged by painters and poets and, in moments of self-revelation, by all of us. The refinement of our perception helps us to increase our knowledge of what we see, just as the study of natural history increases our knowledge of the processes of life all around us. "To a person uninstructed in natural history," wrote Thomas Henry Huxley, "his country or seaside stroll is like a walk through a gallery full of wonderful works of art, nine-tenths of which have their faces turned to the wall."

A real gallery of paintings may increase our knowledge as happily as an informed walk in nature. The conventional aids to painting—linear and aerial perspective, measurements from the picture plane, vanishing points—have all developed from Renaissance art. Conventions not to be observed in earlier European painting or in primitive art are familiar to us in the paintings of the masters of later days, especially in their *veduta* or view paintings. Later in time, one might find a better understanding of what wilderness means in the painters of the Hudson River School, who cherished and depicted it in the early days of the Republic. Even then the threats were many. "They are cutting down all the trees in the beautiful valley on which I have looked so often with a loving eye," lamented the painter Thomas Cole in a letter to the New York merchant Luman Reed describing the coming of the railroad. "Join with me in maledictions on all dollar-godded utilitarians."

Landscape painters have looked at town and countryside in every possible way. They have left nothing unseen. "The contrast between the seventeenth and eighteenth centuries is emphasized by their different conceptions of landscape," writes the art historian Denys Sutton. "For Poussin landscape was a means by which he could reiterate his belief in Classical principles; for Claude a way of providing an escape into a romantic dream world; for Gaspard Dughet an opportunity to delight in the rugged beauties of the Roman campagna; and for Salvator Rosa a chance of evoking the strangeness of nature."* The tourists come in numbers and view painting develops. A typical exponent is Gaspar Van Wittel; the genre flowers in the paintings of Bellotto, Canaletto, and Guardi. In the rebuilding of Warsaw after the second world war, Bellotto's meticulous but picturesque views of the city were used as models, even to the reproduction of exterior ornament.

Our surroundings are being destroyed and we are losing all the qualities of what used to be called "scenery." When a landscape is considered to be "scenic," its esthetic qualities are somehow better served. Only when a proper appreciation of scenery returns can destruction be halted and the esthetic content restored to our cities and countryside, to what we build and to what we plan.

In reviving a love of landscape, we must try to be like that someone who points out the view, someone who recognizes the value of what is to be seen.

* Denys Sutton, "Where the Lemon Trees Blossom," *Apollo* (September 1970), p. 177.

LANDSCAPE AND SCIENCE

Understanding What We See

Science opens many doors to understanding. Where the knowledge of environment is concerned several of the sciences make their contribution. In particular, geology, botany, psychology, and that branch of physics known as optics have much to tell us about our impressions of the world of nature—the limited but rewarding glimpses of the visible universe which our powers afford.

One should begin with a disclaimer, however. It is, of course, not essential to know how and when a river began to flow in order to appreciate its graceful meander or torrential fall. The valley which surrounds it will not necessarily seem any more beautiful to those who know that the river may have been the means of its creation. It is not likely that an ancient Greek had a lesser esthetic appreciation of the Gorge of Tempe than does modern man, just because he supposed it was created by a blow from the trident of Poseidon (a myth rejected by Herodotus, incidentally). Human beings have thrived on mythical interpretations of natural phenomena. After the Romans, Vulcan's rumbling underground workshops were replaced in people's minds by the hellish minions of the Devil as the cause of volcanic action. Many Christians, believing that all of nature was but a creation of God's goodness and grace, knew that it was unwise to question any of the revealed works of the Almighty. As late as the seventeenth century a geologist could be proclaimed a heretic for believing that fossil shells were once a part of living animals or that the ocean had once covered parts of the earth. The diluvialists believed that Noah's Flood answered all possible scientific questions of this kind, an idea reigning supreme until well into the eighteenth century. But no one can deny that the eighteenth century had a well-developed sense of environmental esthetics or that still-important books were written about this matter then.[1]

There have been skeptics in every age who have disregarded the prevailing opinion and whose probings have hastened our accumulation of knowledge of

4

natural phenomena. Such curiosity both in and outside the field of science has yielded results. The art critic Nikolaus Pevsner has told us that John Ruskin and Viollet-le-Duc, both famous for their polemics on art and architecture, were drawn to the subject of geology. Presumably this was because they were both enthusiasts of stone (the latter especially until he became enamored of cast iron), but along the way they gave us most useful insights on matters to do with mountains and rivers. They knew by what means the prospect before them was sculptured, insofar as the latest mid-nineteenth century scientific knowledge could provide the answer.

> The summer's work of 1844, so far from advancing the design of Modern Painters, had thrown me off it—first into fine botany, then into difficult geology.[2]

> After passing the curved rock from which the waterfall leaps into its calm festoons, the cliffs become changed in material, first into thin-bedded blue limestone and then into dark slates and shales, which partly sadden, partly enrich, with their cultivable ruin, all the lower hillsides henceforward to the very gate of Chamouni.[3]

Again, it is not necessary to provide oneself with the most thorough handbook in order to enjoy flowering plants, although identification of local "finds" seems to provide a dimension of satisfaction along with the pleasure of contemplation. Other questions—is the plant native; if not, when was it introduced? is it a rarity (which should arouse an interest in protection)? is it a host plant for other forms of life?—when answered may enlarge our perspective on any particular example. For instance, we know much more about the internal migrations of the Monarch butterfly now that Canadian entomologists, aided by amateurs throughout the Monarch's north-south range in the United States, have bred and banded this handsome creature. With favorable wind-tracks, as in 1968 and 1973, the Monarch has even crossed the Atlantic, and has been spotted in the Scilly Isles and southern England. Its host plant, however, has not been found wild in England, so that one is unlikely to find the Monarch breeding there, whereas

I have learned to find its tiny eggs on the milkweed plants in my Connecticut fields and look at this species with more interest than ever before, just as I can better understand the characteristics of a hybrid tree or shrub when I know the parents that have produced the cross.

John Ruskin's sketch of Alpine formations near Chamonix, from the Ruskin Collection at Yale. Ruskin wrote in *Modern Painters* (chap. 14), "Curved cleavage has taken me years to develop among the *aigulles* of Chamouni. . . . And yet in his very first journey . . . Turner saw it at a glance."

Certainly the science of geomorphology (which used to be called physiography and means the study of the configurations of the earth's surface) has much to offer the student of landscape. As long ago as 1802 geologists postulated that valleys are formed by the streams that flow in them, contradicting the then prevalent idea that they happened catastrophically. Since then, glaciation has been better understood (Goethe was the first to suggest that the earth had long ago been subject to an age of cold) and the behavior of the earth's mantle investigated. Knowledge that the present is the key to the past—the doctrine of uniformitarianism pro-

VIEW OF COTOPAXI (1867) by Frederick Edwin Church. This equatorial free-standing extinct volcano has always been counted among the world's great scenic phenomena. Unlike most of the high Andes at this latitude, which remain green, its noble peak is always covered with snow.

pounded by James Hutton (1726–97)—encouraged a more scientific understanding of the processes of a lively earth, at the same time shaking a prevailing belief in its stability.

Luckily for the preservation of scenic patrimony, an important landform very often is dramatic enough to have been accepted by successive generations as a cultural asset. Famous mountains and lakes (Fujiyama, Lake Louise) are obvious examples. Sometimes, however, very small and less striking landscapes have been cherished. France, with less mountainous scenery than some countries (aside from the area of the Alps), has identified as scenic, views which would be considered modest in parts of the world having wilder and more rugged terrain. For example, the "Suisse Normande" has two stars for scenic attractiveness in Michelin, but North and South Americans as well as inhabitants of most Asian countries, who are used to more spectacular scenery, might find the little river valley rather unexciting, albeit of some geological interest and well-suited to walking and canoeing. Although this region does not yield the alpine views implied by its name, it is important that so modest a landscape, without being large or spectacular, has attracted enough attention to be considered worthy of preservation.

Let us take an example to suit the modern interest in the preservation of wild nature. Bartholomew's Cobble is a small area of only a few acres, consisting of two prominent limestone knolls, in southwestern Massachusetts. The knolls rise abruptly from the placid intervales of the Housatonic River, where cattle graze peacefully on the broad meadows. This is still one of the prettiest bucolic landscapes in the eastern United States and worthy of the brush of an Innes or a Homer. It has a scientific interest as well. About four hundred million years ago, according to geologists, these rocks were folded into the ancient Taconic Mountains and were converted under heat and pressure into tremolite-filled marble and quartzite. They were folded again at a later period. Originating as sedimentary deposits under the sea in the Cambrian and Ordovician periods, these ancient rocks are more resistant to weathering than ordinary marble and limestone, and thus have formed the "cobble." The rocks themselves are not the whole story, however. Over seven hundred species of plant life (including fungi, ferns, and mosses), some very rare, have already been identified there. At last count, the naturalist Hal Borland recorded fifty-two species of fern and fern allies within the perimeter. These, together with the birds and small animals which haunt the woods, are all protected nowadays by the ownership and maintenance of the Massachusetts Trustees of Reservations. Thus the Cobble is visited by hundreds of nature lovers, including specialists from Europe and Japan, who know what they are coming to see.

HIGH WATER ON THE HOUSATONIC RIVER AT BARTHOLOMEW'S COBBLE

Anyone would be drawn to the Cobble because its geological position and configuration are so dramatic, in contrast to the water-meadows below, but it would take an expert geologist to deduce from surface features the remarkable European fault which brings the Devonian rocks above the coal measures as it crosses the valley of the Meuse. At that point the poplar-lined river flows steadily northward as before, with never a hint of the successfully concealed hypogene features below. The surface landscape does not evidence the internal structure in any way that can be seen, although in many other places the fault is easily identified. In the majority of situations, so much has happened to the surface in the way of denudation, hydrospheric action, or other external sculptural agents that we must look mainly to these processes as a key to configuration. Among these is erosion, which has an unpleasant connotation to conservationists but in the geologist's notebook is merely followed by deposition somewhere else, nothing being lost thereby in the sum total of the weathering process.

At the same time it must be stressed that surface features cannot be accounted for without some knowledge of the earth sciences and the changes experienced by the earth's crust, complicated as they are. Rocks have been tilted, folded, compressed, fractured, and displaced. Recent world-formation theories involve the concept of lithospheric plates and the spreading of the sea floor, giving rise to the new global tectonics and theories of continental drift. With such ideas being argued by the sea-floor spreaders (mobilists) and the nondrifters (fixists) another revolution in geological thought is on its way. Meanwhile, less cosmic facts of nature, some recently discovered, some centuries old, allow man to change the face of the land. While the oil geologist estimates the production of a new source in the shale beds of Colorado or the Urals, the producers of that small purple grape that makes the sweet wine known as port understand from long experience that it can only be grown where the schist begins above Regua on the Doura River, and not on the granite hills nearby. Hence the contrasting landscapes of that beautiful region of Portugal, alternately luxuriant and bare.

Geology provides the historical record of the shifts that landscape and climate underwent long before man altered the face of the earth to create its pastoral state. Few survivals of earlier inhabitants can still be seen, although the dendrologist and the ichthyologist can point to still existing ancient forms of life, such as the ginkgo and the coelacanth. Fossil plants and animals provide evidence of climatic changes, while bones and teeth unearthed by anthropologists prove that earlier men roamed the earth with beasts and birds now long disappeared.

Knowledge of the "higher" forms of life was widespread by the eighteenth century; their classification was not as difficult as was that of the more numerous lower forms. But odd myths still perpetuated themselves. A biographer of Linnaeus records that this famous scientist could not accept all of the book of Genesis as true, yet believed the common myth "that in winter the swallows slept upon the bottom of lakes." An 1852 edition of Oliver Goldsmith's *Animated Nature* from my grandfather's library still maintains that there must be some degree of probability to that idea. Yet it does go on to note "the experiment of Frisch, who tied several threads, dyed in water-colours, round the legs of departing swallows." These cooperative birds brought their threads back with them the following summer "in no way damaged in their colour; which they most certainly would, if, during the winter, they had been steeped in water." Another eighteenth-century naturalist believed that swallows wintered on the moon. Yet Linnaeus was one of the founders of modern plant science. He based his botanical system on the reproductive organs of plants. Goethe, noted for his theory of color and other scientific investigations, as late as 1820 professed himself anxious that the chaste souls of women and young people should not be embarrassed by botanical textbooks expounding "the dogma of sexuality."[4] A lesser poet, Erasmus Darwin, made charming fun of the famous system in his "Loves of the Plants." There are probably still people who believe in the mandrake legend, and there are those who assert that plants respond to music and the vibrations of the human voice, a current idea which remains unproven.

We know now where swallows mostly winter. Our communications between various parts of the earth are instantaneous. We understand a little better the impulses and biochronometry of plants and animals. We know how bees employ their sense of direction, how birds navigate, and how plants respond to long and short periods of daylight. Discoveries are made daily on every aspect of the living world, past and present. If we had set out now instead of in the nineteenth century to find the source of the Nile it would not have taken the years of effort, heartbreak, and acrimony that it did, but possibly only a day of aerial exploration or an instant of satellite photography.

Important for the student of landscape is the science of acclimatization, the discovery of and introduction of new species, as well as the breeding of new strains. The last-named activity can change a landscape in short order, as witness the novelty of dry rice cultivation in Indonesia, which does not need the time-honored water-filled paddy. But acclimatization usually proceeds in slower fashion, involving chance and history. It, too, can effect the transformation of a countryside, as witness the introduction of the sugar cane from the Canaries to the West Indies, or, perhaps even more, the influence of the humble potato, *Solanum tuberosum*, which crossed the Atlantic the other way.

The Dissemination of Landscape Material

Seed-bearing plants have ways of travelling by air or water, or they can be carried by birds, but many have never travelled on their own, having rather been brought by man. These have found a home in botanical gardens, where they are studied and adapted for a new life in agriculture, forestry, or food-producing horticulture. These preserves or acclimatization plots often have an esthetic or historical interest far beyond their scientific importance and have become a part of the landscape tradition. Some reflect the private hobbies of the amateur, as witness the establishment of pineta in Europe and America in the nineteenth century.[5] Others have become part of the national patrimony and have played their roles in colonization or in the general advancement of science. Some are curious, but nearly all have the inherited beauty that comes from careful husbandry and age.

If it happens that the oldest botanical garden of all suits the above description best, it is because it was imaginatively laid out in the beginning and has kept its form through the years.[6] It matters little that Pisa is wont to claim first place in time, since the garden at Padua, founded in 1545 by the Venetian Republic, is certainly its contemporary and much more charming, with its beds laid out in imitation of the four quarters of the globe, a little universe crammed full of medicinal and other plants. Under glass one finds the Palma di Goethe, the study of which enabled the poet to write his *Metamorphosis of Plants*. Many of the plants introduced into this garden from Turkey and Asia Minor are now common throughout Europe. Among the people who studied and worked there are many pioneers of botanical science, founders of other gardens in most of the important towns of Italy.

The worldwide traffic in plants which accompanied the age of navigation proliferated botanical gardens and arboreta in towns and universities in the old and new worlds, a process which continues. Today there are over a thousand important ones, some of the more recent having been founded to protect rather than disseminate species. But acclimatization has often been undertaken without their aid. Occasionally plant introduction plays a role in the social history of a continent. We see Franciscans showing the Quito Indians how to plant grain in the great space before the Franciscan monastery, which later became one of the most splendid squares in the Western hemisphere, with its staircase and terrace (after a design by Bramante) and La Compania, the jewelled and gilded church of the Jesuits, built by Moslem workmen, below. All this in a former capital of the Incas, the Andes rising steeply about and the majestic volcano Cotopaxi only thirty-five miles down the valley. Parent nations, however, gained a great deal more from their colonies in the way of landscape material than they ever gave.

Three hundred years after the Spanish invasion of the Americas we see the British convicts and crown squatters facing the unknown in the Australian bush and its literally hundreds of species of Eucalypts. Their naming of these native trees, which nobody had seen elsewhere in the world, was picturesque in the extreme. Broad-leaved Sally, Argyle Apple, Gympie Messmate, Slaty Box, Moitch, Cowcowing Mallee, and Warty Yate are all members of the genus Eucalyptus—the common names of Apple and Box are confusing to the visitor, although not perhaps to Australians. It was not until a protege of Sir William Hooker, Dr. von Müller, born of Danish parents in 1825 (later created an hereditary baron by the king of Wurtemburg), who had sought out Australia for his health, threw himself into the occupation of sorting out the imperfectly classified flora of his adopted land that the ongoing exploration of the botanically difficult family of gums began to make sense.

Müller is interesting for another activity—he was instrumental in introducing the eucalyptus to Italy to aid in the draining of the Pontine marshes, to Abyssinia to provide shade where no other tree would grow, and to California, where the

INSIDE THE ORTO BOTANICO, PADUA. The layout remains much as it was when the Venetian Republic conceived it in 1545. The palm tree, which is said to have inspired Goethe's *Metamorphosis of Plants*, was planted in 1585 and is now protected by its own house (opposite page).

quick-growing *Eucalyptus globosus* was introduced as a timber tree. Except in the colder parts of the globe, these gray-green trees with their constantly drooping foliage, appearing so melancholy by the mile in Australia, and definitely an acquired but attractive taste for the landscape lover, provide a fascinating contrast to the native sylva when introduced elsewhere, as anyone who has travelled through Morocco, where several species flourish and have been extensively planted as forest and roadside trees, can testify. There they obtain a good size and a reasonable outline, whereas in the Caribbean climate of the Jamaican botanical garden of Cinchona, at 5,000 feet, they are veritable giants. At Cinchona there are about nine species of gums out of a reputed Australian cadre of seven hundred.

It is on the same island that a tiny botanical garden, now reduced by flood erosion to an acre or less, has the most romantic story of all to tell. This is at Bath, in the southwestern part of Jamaica, where its establishment was ordered by a statute of 1774. The garden came into being five years later. Bath is only a little later in time than the botanical garden at Saint Vincent, which claims to be the oldest extant botanical garden in the Western hemisphere and is also small, with a great deal of interest and charm. The garden at Bath was established under the aegis of its superintendent Dr. Thomas Clarke, who was a physician at the nearby hot springs (which still have their devotees). It was well-stocked with Chinese and Indian importations—teas, camphor, litchie, sago palms, jujube, clove, and the Chinese dragon tree. Here, in June 1782, came the contents of the well-named H. M. S. *Flora*, which, under Lord Rodney, had captured a French ship on its way to Haiti from the Indian Ocean with a cargo of plants including the mango, cinnamon, jak-fruit, pandanus, moringa, and oriental ebony. The admiral brought this valuable live catch to Bath, where at least one of the original specimens, the screw pine, can still be seen. A few years later Captain Bligh brought Jamaica's staff of life, the breadfruit, from Tahiti, on his second and less eventful journey there.[7]

The smaller botanical gardens are usually rewarding and easily comprehended. The most famous in England is the Apothecaries' Garden in Chelsea, established in 1673 and granted in 1722 to the Society of Apothecaries by Sir Hans Sloane, who had also been in Jamaica. The "Physic Garden" is now run by a committee of management. The gardens of Oxford and Cambridge are also well known. Less familiar, although now frequented by thousands of tourists annually, is the botanical garden at Orotona in the Canary Islands, founded in 1788 by the marquis of Villanueva del Prado, a litterateur and botanist of local fame, to acclimatize plants from the Spanish possessions overseas. It is a walled enclosure on a hillside, with a formal layout of great charm and interest, where peacocks spread their fans and the indigenous devil tree its curious head of leaves.

Apart from "physic" gardens, the first true botanic garden in what is now the United States was John Bartram's in Philadelphia, the site of which is well worth a visit, though not especially for the trees, which have mostly succumbed in the grime of the surrounding industrial development, but for the house, designed by Bartram in the classical manner in 1731.[8] The earliest in New York, excluding the physic gardens of New Amsterdam, was Dr. David Hosack's Elgin Botanic Garden, now the site of Rockefeller Center. It was "a repository of native plants" and was famous for its neoclassic conservatory, a sketch of which by John Trumbull is in the Yale University Art Gallery. Harvard established its botanical garden in 1807. Specialized botanical gardens now abound; one can find them for desert plants in Arizona and for subtropical species in Florida and Louisiana. The Fairchild Tropical Garden's Palmetum in Florida is the focus of the largest collection of palms and cycads to be found anywhere.

By the nineteenth century almost any city of importance had its botanical garden or park, many of them adding to their primary purpose the facilities of a pleasure ground. The Jardin des Plantes in Paris is a delightful addition to the Left Bank for this reason as well as for its taxonomic importance. The Jardin des Plantes in Nantes is frankly laid out as a public promenade, with elaborate lakes and waterfalls, rocks, grottoes, and artificial adornments, as well as a handsome avenue of magnolias. Purists may regret the emphasis on pleasure, but who is to say that the *promenade* is not serious, especially for French grandmothers and their young charges, as well as for lovers everywhere (even though the *promenade en auto* has usurped this function in the United States).

It is the combination of scientific and esthetic interest that makes the botanic garden such an intriguing subject for landscape study. It deserves more attention than it receives for its provisions for both recreation and wildlife preservation,

In 1806 the celebrated historical painter John Trumbull made a pencil sketch of Dr. Hosack's greenhouses, in the latter's Elgin Botanic Garden, on the site of what is now Rockefeller Center. It was the first garden of its kind in New York.

both of which are more popular today and have become overriding forces in the creation of new open space. But what could be more fascinating as open space than an ancient botanical garden planted on the site of old fortifications in the center of Zurich, or that city's arboretum on the lakeside, with all its trees carefully labelled and illustrated descriptions provided of the water birds that frequent the place to be fed by the townspeople? The sedate walkers in the

Dolderthal woods high up above the town commune with nature differently, their eyes anxiously watching dogs unleashed, and bent exclusively on a Sunday afternoon's exercise.

The botanical collection is becoming a prime tourist attraction, as attendance figures at Bogor near Djakarta and in Singapore, among dozens of lesser places, have recorded. Of national parks and forest reserves we shall speak later; meanwhile, let us return to Australia to absorb the lesson of Melbourne's botanic garden, founded by Charles Joseph La Trobe, of the well-known Huguenot family which produced Benjamin Henry Latrobe, one of the architects of the United States Capitol. Charles Joseph had travelled in America too, with Washington Irving, and had pronounced its scenery "sublime" in his book *A Rambler in North America*. For the eventual botanical garden he chose a site on marshy land on the south bank of the Yarra River. He appointed the first director of the gardens in 1846, while he was still superintendent of the little colony at Port Philip (he was later made lieutenant governor of Victoria).[9]

The aforementioned onetime director Baron von Müller wanted to develop the place as a strictly scientific institution, "a living textbook of systematic and economic botany." He ignored any possible need for lawns and thought the lake a useful spot for the dumping of rubbish. No wonder Anthony Trollope wrote (in 1873):

> The gardens of Adelaide cannot rival those of Sydney,—which, as far as my experience goes, are unrivalled in beauty anywhere. Nothing that London possesses, nothing that Paris has, nothing that New York has, comes near to them in loveliness. In Melbourne the gardens are more scientific, but the world at large cares but little for science. In Sydney the public gardens charm as poetry charms. At Adelaide they please like a well-told tale. The gardens at Melbourne are as a long sermon from a great divine—whose theology is unanswerable, but his language tedious.[10]

The world-famous baron was eased out of his job as director and in an embittered old age would never set foot in the gardens again. He was followed by one

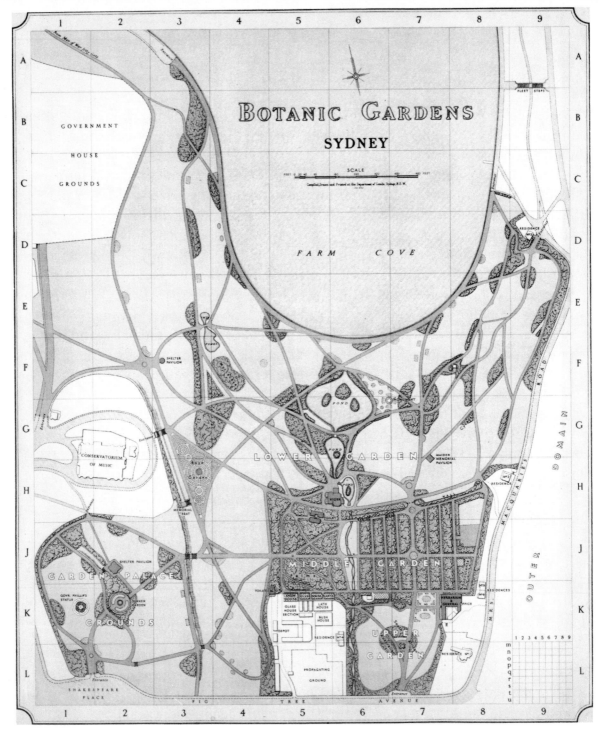

Plan of the Royal Botanical Gardens on Sydney Harbor. In 1873 Anthony Trollope called them the most beautiful he had seen, far surpassing anything in New York, London, or Paris. The collection of cycads is the envy of many another like institution, but the gardens also blossom with bedding displays, now as then much enjoyed by Sydneysiders. When Trollope was in Melbourne a controversy over floral displays was at its height, the public demanding more of them in its botanical garden, which had hitherto been devoted strictly to scientific pursuits. The public won.

William Guilfoyle, who had an artistic eye and who enlarged the property, creating the lush plantings and vistas that we see today. He was incidentally responsible for making the now Royal Botanic Gardens of Melbourne on the Yarra River an incomparable social asset in the midst of a sea of metropolitan growth. Guilfoyle's motto was "There's always something interesting around the corner,"[11] which a visit to the gardens today, when the trees are at maturity, proves correct. The views of the lake, framed by exotic foliage, are superb. The Melbourne gardens cannot surpass Sydney's for the latter's magnificent site on the world's most scenic harbor, but they have just as artfully displayed their wares, proving that beauty and utility contribute most when hand-in-hand.

A relatively new, tropical example is the Pacific Tropical Botanical Garden at Lawai, Hawaii, chartered by Act of Congess in 1964. It will eventually be joined with the adjacent gardens started by Queen Emma, wife of Kamehameha; she was a great plant lover and lived in that spot until 1875. The Pacific Ocean, in fact, is rich in botanical gardens, a particularly charming small one being found near the Gauguin Museum in Tahiti. As for Japan, that nation of plant and flower enthusiasts, it is a home of specialized collections, as well as of the more conventional European-type botanical gardens such as the one in Kyoto, started in 1917. The Fuji Botanical Garden is devoted exclusively to bamboo. One may find in Hasadera a famous peony garden, while at Sukagawa, north of Tokyo, is another, with several hundred specimens over two hundred years old. There are half a hundred noted cherry resorts in Japan, where from the unfolding of the flowers to petal fall there is always somebody watching; and even some individual trees in Japan are classed as national monuments.

The Royal Botanic Garden at Godavari, 16 kilometers from Kathmandu, is located at the base of the Pulchowki ("flower") Mountain, which rises up to 2,715 meters from sea level and is the highest in the valley. The atmospheric and soil conditions allow for a wide range of subtropical and temperate zone flora. A stream runs through the garden; there are a fish farm and sacred ponds just above; and a varied topography in the little valley enlivens the landscape design. Apart from the outdoor displays, scientific horticulture is carried on under glass in cactus, orchid, and other greenhouses on terraces.

In spite of the fact that the garden was only started in 1962, it already contains thousands of specimens, while a large herbarium and office building to house the staff and collections of the Department of Medicinal Plants is almost completed. Nepal has been supplying its neighbors and the world with medicinal herbs for at least 2,000 years and these products still form a large part of her export trade.

The garden is easily reached by good roads. School children are brought there in buses for botanical study. There is a road up the mountain which passes a marble quarry and an interesting temple complex; with improvement it could be used as access to the native floral habitat and scenic views of the entire valley. The mountain is a familiar place to the Nepalese, a pilgrimage spot which was once covered with a dense forest. The demand for fuel in urban districts has removed some of the forest, but much remains, and the forest is now protected by law. Rhododendron species are a particular glory of the hillsides in spring, and orchids, ferns, clematis, jasmin, and other plants grow on the forest floor.

Advances in horticulture have introduced floral displays into city parks as well as botanic gardens, a typical example being St. James's Park in London. In this century, too, such horticultural parks as Wisley Gardens (the Royal Horticultural Society's trial grounds) have attracted thousands of visitors, many of whom come to study the plantings as well as to admire. Developments on hybridization, too, have created gardens devoted to a single family of plants. Interest in the rose, far and away the favorite flower of Western man, has inspired the splendid Roseraie at l' Haÿ les Roses near Paris, the trial grounds at Bagatelle (formerly used for riding practice by the Prince Imperial), Queen Mary's rose garden in Regent's Park, and the Brooklyn Botanic Garden, to name only a few specialized places. There is a fascinating hillside devoted entirely to lilac species and hybrids at Rochester, New York, where at the right moment in May one can wander through a mist of mauve, pink, and purple, enveloped in that heady perfume, with the great trusses nodding overhead.

In Boulogne-sur-Seine, a small park, now owned by the city of Paris but begun between 1895 and 1900 as a private pleasure ground by Albert Kahn, a former pupil of Bergson turned financier, combines horticultural interest with a series of planned out-of-door pictures—French, English, and Japanese gardens, an alpine garden, a "blue forest" (chiefly of *Cedrus atlantica glauca* and Koster's blue spruce), a "golden forest" (mainly *Picea excelsa aurea*), a "forest of the Vosges," and so on. It is sometimes used as a place for official garden parties, with musicians hidden in a palmarium. During long-ago nocturnal receptions, an early electrical installation would illuminate successive garden scenes as the guests wandered through them, leaving other parts of the grounds in darkness. It is still a charming place, full of interest and surprises, some of which were originally planned by the well-known *architecte paysagiste* Duchesne, and although the original care invested by thirty-six gardeners is no longer apparent, as it was when Clemenceau and the Prince of Wales visited them during the first world war, the Jardins Kahn reflect a winning artifice not to be found in many of the present-day horticultural gardens and parks.

Scientific investigation proceeds apace, keeping up with agricultural research in all areas. A botanical garden can be an exotic fantasy like Kew, with buildings designed in the "Chinese" manner by Sir William Chambers, and remain the great scientific institution it always was. Another laboratory devoted to the latest scientific research is the New York Botanical Garden, whose board believes that "contemplation of flower beds and greenhouse exotica will hardly satisfy the new generation."[12] This botanic garden is a research center for organismal biology, its practitioners contrasting their occupation with "the intense biochemical professionalism" of many university departments. Studies of algae and plankton there have opened new chapters in limnology and oceanography. There is talk of equipping "the new class of cultivars" with recently developed scientific tools to trace the movements of algae and flagellates for clues in the current investigations into the nature of life—a new occupation for our leisure time. All this from an urban botanical garden.[13]

Apart from biological research, a new role for botanical gardens closely related to our pursuit of landscape appreciation is conservation of the world's flora. This goes beyond their "museum" function, and beyond the role that many, like the new garden at Canberra, have already adopted, that of collector of native flora. The new role is the safeguarding of stocks of threatened species, reflecting John and William Bartram's pioneer discovery and subsequent propagation of the

Franklinia, not found in the wild after 1803, but now an adornment of many a southern garden. The Cambridge Botanical Garden now has stocks of over fifty rare species of British wild origin, including the only known clump of a sedge, *Schoenus ferrugineus*, that has been extinct in Britain since the construction of a reservoir in Scotland.[14] This form of conservation is as important for the future as is the preservation of wild nature in situ.

The naturalist Aldo Leopold has said that the difference between a botanical garden, where everything is arranged, and a wilderness is that the latter induces humility in man. Humility or no, the botanical garden induces scientific curiosity, and often, as we have seen, it encourages esthetic sensibilities which are an important contribution to the cultural development of mankind. And they are very precious examples of man's dedication to the furtherance of useful and peaceful knowledge. Like nature reserves and wilderness areas, they form oases which testify to man's determination to husband nature in the midst of the growing complexities of modern life.

Productive Landscapes

Older by far than scientific biological knowledge, and of paramount importance in the fashioning of landscapes, are the practices of agriculture and forestry. Here we are concerned with technique, which comes before science—if we are to believe a recent challenge to the traditional view that technique is an application of science.[15] Even primitive man was acquainted with certain techniques, "and the first techniques of Hellenistic civilization were Oriental; they were not derived from Greek science."[16] Today all scientific research presupposes enormous technical preparation and the relationship has become blurred.

One can agree that the techniques of husbandry have grown up without any particular reliance on science, at least in their pre-Mendelian stages. Planting by the phases of the moon, dowsing for well-digging, or ploughing a furrow around the site for a new town may have some scientific connotations, but they were not practiced by men with scientific minds. The seasonal activities of agriculture which vary in different parts of the globe were largely a matter of folklore until the

WILDERNESS IN TOWN. This view of the Bronx River Gorge (part of the New York Botanical Garden) was taken by an unknown photographer in 1895.

seventeenth century; they accelerated with the invention of mechanized farm equipment at the time of the American Civil War. Man knew the value of irrigation and how to make earth dams and dikes long before he understood the dynamics of engineering science. The husbandman has always been a traditionalist, and his methods, often wasteful of energy but usually essentially practical, for centuries preserved an agricultural stability, and with it many familiar or easily recognized aspects of the countryside.

Technical progress and the agricultural revolution changed all this. We have seen with our own eyes the ploughing up of the American prairie, the pastoralists' practice of overgrazing the formerly lush hillsides of New Zealand, as well as the cutting down of the hedges and home orchards of Normandy farmers since France entered the European Communities. While in the past forest usually gave way to farmland, especially after the breakdown of the feudal system, with its lords of the hunt, nowadays in Western Europe unproductive farmland gives way to forest under the Mansholt Plan, as it did in marginal areas of the Tennessee Valley under the New Deal.

Not all the changes adversely affect landscape values, in spite of British complaints that the Forestry Commission has too great a penchant for clothing the slopes of Scotland and Westmoreland with somber conifers, or American protests against the clear-cutting methods of private forest industry. In recent years attempts at amenity have marked some forest practices, and while there is no need to go as far as a forester in the Lake District who has planted his trees in shapes to imitate clouds, there have been advances in mixed plantings and the provision of views. Quite recently efforts have been made to plant trees in patterns that will be pleasing to the motorist.

Attitudes to the treed landscape have varied over the years. The American pioneers' slash-and-burn methods did far more damage to North American forests than anything the Native Americans had done. In Australia there is a humorous saying, "If it moves, shoot it; if it grows, cut it down," but the same thing could be said of North America once. When George Perkins Marsh wrote his now-famous work *Man and Nature: Physical Geography as Modified by Human Action* over one hundred years ago, he could say that the laws of almost every European state more or less adequately ensured the permanence of the forest, mentioning that Spain then was the only European land which had not made some public provision for the protection and restoration of its woods. Sadly he added, "The vast forests of the United States and Canada cannot long resist the unprovident habits of the backwoodsman and the increased demand for lumber." New uses for wood, the growth of newspapers and hydrocarbon chemical industries, as well as the exporting of lumber to other countries, have not yet depleted the forests to a critical point, but who can say that the insatiable maw of industry will not precipitate a catastrophe if it is not further restrained by the government. Yet in North America there is still real wilderness. Perhaps the most sophisticated approach to forest management is that of recent wilderness preservation, where fallen trees are left to rot, renewing the soil, and the only major changes take place through the agencies of fire or flood.

Marsh was a keen observer of the landscape, noting that the winter scene in Italy is enhanced by the presence of so many evergreens. "Indeed it is only in the winter," he goes on to say, "that a tourist who confines himself to wheeled carriages and high roads can acquire any notion of the face of the earth, and form any proper geographical image of that country. . . . The frequency of the cypress and the (umbrella) pine—combined with the fact that the other trees of Southern Europe which most interest a stranger from the north, the orange and the lemon, the cork oak, the ilex, the myrtle and the laurel are evergreens— goes far to explain the beauty of the winter scenery of Italy."[17]

While American ambassador to the new kingdom of Italy, Marsh noted that the planting of 36,000 eucalypts had helped to dry up the Roman marshes.[18] He combined an intense scientific curiosity with an admiration of the natural world and was described characteristically by Matthew Arnold as "that rara avis, a really well-bred and trained American." In taste he was more like Thoreau than Ruskin, whose criticisms he despised as too "arty," saying that the former had articulated a great many facts of natural history through observation which had later been proved correct by scientific method. Marsh has been overlooked in the current effort to make Frederick Law Olmsted the hero of the environmentalists. He is nonetheless the real father of the conservation movement in the United States, if only because of his penetrating analysis of man's carelessness with the land.

Marsh loved the natural forests of his native Vermont, and had seen them mismanaged and denuded. But he was not averse to artificial planting of new forests or to great technological achievements like the draining of the Zuyder Zee. "Restore and maintain the earth" was his motto. Marsh was concerned, as we must be, with both the man-made and the man-ravaged landscape. "A middle aged man returning to the scenes of his childhood," he said, "will not be observing the same things that he saw then." Any former resident of Florida or the Costa del Sol could corroborate this statement, or any traveller to Japan after a ten-year absence.

Many of Marsh's precepts have become the lore of the environmentalists, who have checked mismanagement and have increasingly halted violent abuse of the landscape. An obvious example is the current interest in the importance of wetlands, which Marsh said acted like a sponge to regulate the waters, and which is reflected in laws being enacted in many countries to prevent the destruction of mangrove and phragmites swamps in the tropical Pacific and graminoid marshes in the north Atlantic. Supposed in Marsh's day to be only of interest to the occasional sportsman and in ours to landfill operators and marina promoters, wetlands have been shown by science to support vital forms of aquatic life and to be a valuable environment for hydrological control measures.

Examples of unique species to be found in wetlands are numerous. The rare long-toed salamander is an amphibian that breeds only in one small marsh in Santa Cruz, California. This was to be filled and made into a trailer park until conservation groups protested and biologists testified that the five-inch long beast had had rights of possession for ten to twenty thousand years.[19] Another is the tailor bird, which in Australia is believed to nest only in one small piece of swampy, scrubby ground next to a golf course in Dee Why, near Sydney. Protests mounted a few years ago when it was learned that the town wished to take the land for a sports field. Many of the world's important breeding grounds are quite small and therefore vulnerable to almost any change in land use. An unusual example of pastoral preservation is to be found among the new buildings of the University of Victoria on Vancouver Island, where, owing to the protests of students and faculty, a large, rough piece of grassland has been kept in the middle of the campus, unmowed and inviolate. Until recently it was the only breeding ground in North America of the imported English skylark, which can be heard trilling overhead all summer long. The adoption by all societal groups of ecological thinking is the most welcome surprise of the postwar world.[20]

It cannot be overemphasized that conservation of landscape (and hence of all landscape values) is a social and economic question, over which the scientist has little control. It is too easy to blame technology, still worse to rely on it to solve social and economic problems. An example of such reliance is the invention and installation of machines for the depuration of shellfish near the source of supply, when the origin of the trouble lies not in the waters of the bay but in some manufacturing plant upstream. The oysterman, caught in a trap not of his own making, has recourse to technology only in desperation. An ecological approach would solve his problem, but this is a matter for society, and no discreet application of science is sufficient.

It is not my intention here to analyze the ecological approach. Its methods, which challenge the older scientific methods of investigation by isolating the phenomena, are at last becoming accepted. It is perhaps more important here to inquire into man's relationship to his landscapes. Political scientist Lynton Caldwell asks whether the most promising organizing concept (for study) is to view the phenomenon of man ecologically or to study natural systems with reference to man, the latter being the conventional homocentric approach.[21] The question provokes another: Is man a part of all he sees or a spectator only, studying landscapes as Burckhardt advised his readers to study history, as one would contemplate a storm at sea, safe on the shore? Should we not be terrified that the storm may touch *us*? Are we not involved, emotionally and physically, in nature, and is not our role one far more deeply committed than that of mere guardianship or good behavior toward the wild? The Judaeo-Christian image of man as lord of the earth and only responsible to a higher power for his actions still dominates our behavior toward animals and plants. Thoreau's admonition to man to be modest because "earth has higher uses than we put her to" must only be reinforced by scientific advance, not diminished in import, and the death of a species considered a crime for which no compensation can be given and none received, and for which no expiation will suffice.

The lesson is the shared environment. The varying cultural values, plurality of interests, and multiplicity of life requirements demand a rich and elaborate matrix in which to flourish—an environment of high quality, in fact. Ecology embraces the single blade of grass, but it also operates on the scale of the river valley, the mountain range, and the hydrosphere, not merely codifying but emphasizing the desirable. Such an approach is vital to the maintenance of future habitats.

Technocracy and Science

Civilization in the grip of technique (in Ellul's sense of the word) is nowhere manifested so dramatically as in the advance of the automobile. Personalized transportation on rubber tires, once a toy of the middle class, has over the years created its own demands and run wild like quicksilver over the land, so that no part of life is unaffected by its presence. For one thing, the automobile has

A Colonial Road in New England. These often fascinating byways are subject to dire threats: abandonment or sale by town governments or make-work projects of road widening which destroy the bordering vegetation.

spawned a type of road that suits its characteristics (and indeed is found to have a lower accident rate than former roads)—the limited access highway. When H. G. Wells wrote in 1902 of the possibility of new roads, "There is no reason why the essential charm of the country should disappear; the new roads will not supersede the present high roads, which will still be necessary for horses and subsidiary traffic,"[22] he was underestimating the potential of the new form of transportation, which could go anywhere and which was to account later for road widening and replacement in the name of safety, as the engine became more powerful and the "citizen's car" after 1912 was mass-produced in millions. Foreseeing the growth of the urban region, Wells nevertheless thought that "all that is pleasant and fair of our present countryside may still be there among the other things," but he lived to see all village life destroyed on the trunk roads leading out of London. In the United States by 1927 this could be written:

> One cannot be too emphatic about the necessity of bad roads, for they are the town's defensive rampart and home guard, without which it goes very rapidly the melancholy way that nearly all good trout streams have gone, and for the same reason. It is chiefly because the roads have been not quite bad enough that the present eulogy so narrowly misses being an elegy. The direst foe of the little town is not storm or fire or flood, but gasoline; it can weather the centuries bravely and its old age is healthier than its youth, but it suddenly crumbles and falls, like Jericho, at the sound of the horn.[23]

The landscape connoisseurs were well equipped to forecast the changes that the automobile age would bring. Writing in 1904 on "The Motor-Car and the Genius of Places," the critic Vernon Lee, whose interest in esthetic theory led her to extensive behavioral analysis, speculated on the time when the car would be within the reach of many. It would end the degradation of being conveyed like cattle (on the railway), she thought, and there were other experiences it would afford, such as a sense of triumph over steepness and the ability to see great tracts of land. However, she did not find that driving heightened her sense of topography (it was lessened, in fact—smoothed out), and there was a lack of tangible joy in its fleeting impressions, in which "the corroborative evidence of my limbs" was missing. "The dream-land whirls past and makes little difference to me," she concluded, as if to underscore the alienation that modern man would suffer in ever-increasing ways.

How like the experience of today's automobile driver, now being analyzed extensively (but not any more perceptively) by behavioral scientists. In one such study it was discovered by analyzing drivers' behavior that their view seldom extended much beyond the roadside and that at intersections and interchanges they had very little opportunity to view the landscape because of the complications and hazards of driving. They tended to concentrate on the road ahead and on surrounding traffic.

So much for the joys of motoring today. But if the landscape is not ideally seen by automobile drivers, at least we now know how they react to certain stimuli. In an exhaustive study of perception through behavior, M. K. Vernon concludes that perception is increased by knowledge, an idea which has been explored by art historian Bernard Berenson, among others. In *Seeing and Knowing*, an essay written toward the end of a long life taken up mainly with these two activities, Berenson pointed out, "What we generally call seeing is a utilitarian convention, built up in the race since it has been human and perhaps when still higher animal; and in individuals of today by all sorts of contacts and conditionings to which we are submitted during the years prior to self-awareness." [24] There is a compromise between seeing and knowing, he says, which is a compromise between retinal vision and conceptual looking. It is important to realize that the latter plays its part in comprehending what we see.

Perception as a function of expectations is a relatively new concept, evolved on the part of psychologists to fill gaps left by dissatisfaction with Gestalt psychology and the "behaviorist stimulus-response" theories of B. F. Skinner, which do not appear to fit many everyday activities. [25] Here "memory" (hence history) enters the picture and similarities between objects and events are related to the situation of the moment. Thus identification may include more than the senses perceive at the time. Such a concept would give much more importance to already-seen landscapes in the evaluation of views in city or country.

Recent work in optics reveals that in observing an object the eye follows "scan paths" moving about between fixed points. This has been discovered by recording eye movements, which, interestingly, travel around the same object on different paths for each individual. It is assumed that individuals store these scan paths in the memory for all seen objects. Perception then goes beyond available sensory data (for example, one knows there is a back to a head seen face-on). Thus the brain has stored information derived from past situations which allows it to choose among possibilities. [26]

If the eye can often be misled, physics can explain the error. And illusion is not always a bad substitute for reality. In winter, my eye tells me that the gray, cloud-covered sky is darker than the brilliant snow scene all around me. It is the sky from which the light comes and the illuminated surface of the snow cannot

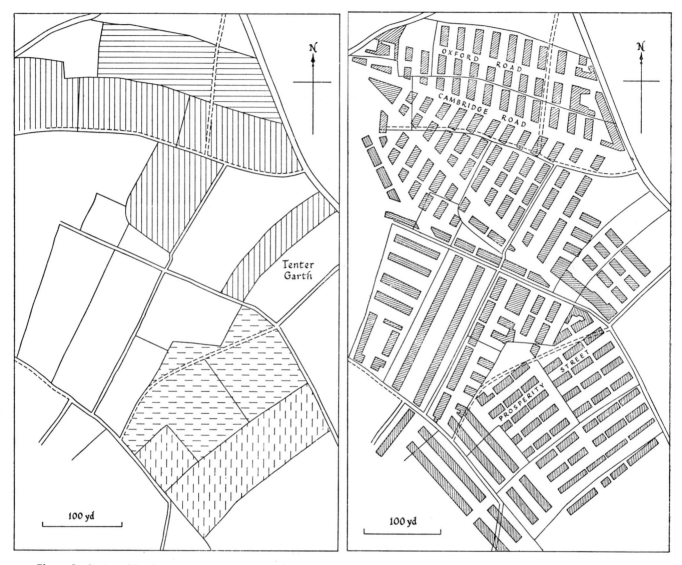

Plans of a district of Leeds, England, before and after development, showing how a street pattern can evolve from fields and lanes.

have a greater brightness than the source. This can be proved by a photometer. Yet the intense whiteness of the snow is not diminished for me, because it is infinitely brighter than the dark trees and other terrestrial objects in my view.[27]

Observing the "green flash" at sunset from a ship in the Caribbean, if one is lucky enough to experience the right atmospheric conditions, inevitably produces a desire to know its origin. A mirage effect is present; again the eye is not seeing things exactly as they are. Who would not gain an inner satisfaction and pleasure from relating the vision to its scientific explanation? The relationship of cause and effect in the landscape is not limited to understanding of luminosity, color, and the values of shadows, which received great attention in Ruskin's *Modern Painters*, a book demonstrating, among other things, a surprisingly accurate observation of such natural phenomena, including that of aquatic reflections.

The understanding of what we see has been furthered in the years since World War II, by new disciplines, especially in the social sciences. Urban geography is one. Another is economic history, which only became academically respectable after 1928, according to M. W. Beresford, when Cambridge University appointed a professor in that subject.[28] Interestingly enough, Professor Beresford's own approach to economic history is visual. He places his emphasis on those visible remains by which past economic activity can be detected. In his inaugural lecture at Leeds he pointed out the manner in which that city's urban landscape was created out of a preexistent pattern of fields. He showed why the parish church was placed where it is, away from the marketplace, and why some streets are straight and some crooked.

To be able to recognize such phenomena is a pleasure to be gained from studying architectural styles and city-planning history. It is certainly important to be able to classify other types of landscape than those which can be identified through the natural sciences. The urban geographer has been of great help to us here. He has shown how classes of towns arose, how certain parts of towns exhibit like characteristics, and why certain functions occur on the fringes, others at the center. He focuses on *location*, and that, in the real world, is a great advance on the older method of categorizing towns, which was far too often just a descriptive gazeteer of their contents and principal buildings.[29]

We have spoken of the specialist-historian, but actually all those who favor a historical model can contribute further to our understanding of the landscape. We can follow Prosper Mérimée around France, where, as inspector general of historic monuments, he advises us where to look for the best medieval work: "Only where the people were religious, the clergy rich, and the feudal overlords fond of lavish things."[30] Or read the geologist Sir Archibald Geikie, in *Landscape in History*, telling us what happened in southeast England to create the white cliffs of Dover, and proving that science is not hostile to the fancy and the imagination in his essay on the origins of scenery in the British Isles.[31] All those who use history as a guide, including the knowing ones who use the present as a clue to the past, may add to our understanding. A historical novelist, a landscape poet, a historian of art—these mark the spot "where culture has intruded upon nature, gaining a new foothold for man." Next we shall explore the impact that these artists have made on our view of nature and the land itself.

Grind of Navir – Passage forced by the sea through rocks of hard porphyry   Engd by R Scott Edin.

SCOTTISH WATER-WORN ROCKS.

LANDSCAPE AND ART

Painters of Nature

Can art, like science, aid us in better understanding the environment? Can the powers of art implant a more perfect model of the landscape in the human psyche?

It has been said that Dutch painters gave the English their love of landscape. Even if it is only one among several influences, this kind of transference is important in the formation of man's attitudes, careless or concentrated, toward the love and protection of natural and artificial scenery.

We have spoken briefly of perception and the art of seeing. Turning now to interpretations of the landscape, we find that there are close connections between our attitudes to what we see in the landscape and the arts of painting and literature, including poetry. Painting has had in some ways a more direct influence, but this influence has exhibited changing forms and has been subject to a variety of interpretations.

The very word *landscape* was introduced as a painter's technical term: "The cunning Painter, . . . limning a Land-scape, various, rich and rare."[1] This is not to say that the mode did not exist long before, in societies adhering to a nonanthropomorphic philosophy of nature. Such societies were the Hellenistic-Roman and the Chinese (the latter under the influence of Confucianism and Taoism rather than the anthropomorphic imagery of Buddhist art). Roman painters of the time of Augustus popularized landscape scenes in their mural decorations for private houses. The landscapes depicted were not always mere stylized backgrounds for mythological stories but were often the main theme.[2] They have in common with some Chinese landscapes a way of introducing the spectator into the picture by, among other techniques, bringing the foreground down to his feet. Landscape painting does not appear in Europe again as an independent art form until the sixteenth century, whereas from the eighth century on Chinese land-scape painting is topographical and descriptive, as well as symbolically representative of the seasons or "directions." "Travel landscapes" typical of late medieval Europe appear in China in the tenth and eleventh centuries.[3] At least from the tenth century there is a penetrating observation of nature, as Buddhism begins to fade as the dominant influence in Chinese life. Sherman Lee describes the principles: large trees must rest on solid ground and "far-away figures have no eyes." Further, he shows photographs of Chinese mountain and river scenes which echo their painted images, making those paintings seem less mannered to Western eyes. The great painters of the Tang and Sung dynasties were inspired by the spectacular landscapes of the Li River, where thousands of water-worn rock formations jutting upward like "bluejade hairpins" (a description given to them a thousand years ago) are complemented by lush vegetation, willow trees, and bamboo groves.[4] *Vide* Wang Lee (fourteenth century) as quoted by Siren: "As long as I did not know the form of the Hua Mountain, how could I make a picture of it?" To us, the compositional effects of Chinese painting of all periods may seem arbitrary, but that is because we are conditioned to seeing nature through the eyes of nineteenth-century Western artists, who painted when the landscape genre had become the favored form not only of the aristocracy, as in China, but of the entire class spectrum of industrial society.

Knotted trees and fantastic rock formations, common in Chinese landscapes, are found in the art of Dürer and Leonardo da Vinci. Kenneth Clark ascribes the Western tradition of jagged rocks to Byzantine iconography, which represents Sinai in this way. These "ideograms" for mountains continue into the quat-trocento, but there they echo best the late Gothic style in architecture and decoration. They bear no symbolic relation whatever to the mountains in Chinese landscape paintings, which Chinese artists deemed an expression of "human-heartedness," while late Gothic European painters like Grünewald and Altdorfer found in them a convenient depiction of the horrors of hell and the frequent savagery of life on earth.

These iconographic mountains gradually disappeared, and with them disap-peared a limited way of composing a painting which had forced the artist to take a

bird's-eye view of the landscape, lest the terrain, seen from ground level, threaten to shut out the background.[5] Altdorfer broke this tradition by setting his horizon deep down and adhering to one point of view, while Netherlandish painters were still fixing it rather high. But even though the Alpine world is viewed with a shudder well into the seventeenth century, and painting showed large figures against small backgrounds, we can believe with critic Max Friedlander that "the

LANDSCAPE WITH FIGURES. Central portion of Hans Memling's *Triptych* (1484), originally in the chapel of St. Christopher in Bruges's Church of St. Jacques and now in one of that city's museums. On one side of the saint is St. Maurus reading, and on the other St. Egidius with the doe—giant, elongated figures all, shown against fantastic rock formations.

←— LANDSCAPE WITHOUT FIGURES. Albrecht Altdorfer of Regensburg (c. 1485–1538) was one of the earliest painters of landscapes that reflected a new feeling for nature which would become fashionable among painters later in the sixteenth century. This one is entitled *Landscape with a Footbridge*. Trees now form a forest wall, intermingling their foliage, instead of standing alone and evenly spaced in a mythological wood. Altdorfer's horizon is set low, while his contemporaries in the Netherlands were still setting theirs quite high.

visual arts paved the way for the enjoyment of reality which came later, and gradually educated people into lingering delightedly among the majesties of nature."[6]

Northern artists developed an interest in landscape painting in the fifteenth and sixteenth centuries. In France the manner develops into a major art in the seventeenth century. Earlier attempts to create a natural feeling and verisimilitude in painting are a product of the inventive minds of early Renaissance Florentines.

Art never quarrels with science, in spite of the arbitrary division of the two worlds by C. P. Snow. Science lends its tools to the artist, who takes advantage of them if he is enterprising. The pursuit of science banishes ignorance, but does not necessarily lessen civility and good taste, as Bernard de Fontenelle (1657–1757) observed in his preface to *The Utility of Mathematics and Physics* (1702). In any case, it was the exploration of new artistic values in the Florentine Renaissance which brought with it the discovery of scientific perspective, virtually unused before the fifteenth century, although nonscientific forms such as parallel perspective, combined with the already mentioned high viewpoint, were in use in China long before. One-point or central-point perspective permits spatial extension into depth; it is "visual geometry." It was discovered by Brunelleschi and Alberti; Donatello's *Feast of Herod* (1435), with its base line divided into nine units, follows Alberti's method in paint. The centric point does not appear in Flemish painting until the late fifteenth century; the northern advance toward realism was achieved without its use.

Alberti the theorist was not merely a provider of visual illusions and the inventor of a new way of painting. In *Della Pittura* he writes, "Let us always take from nature what we wish to paint and we will always fashion the most beautiful things." No serious observer of landscapes can miss the implications of that statement.

Even geometrical perspective may not provide a completely accurate account of our visual perceptions.[7] Objects near the eye do not follow its laws (a fact exploited by Cézanne), yet central perspective does transmit to the knowing eye the same arrangements and "distribution of light" as does the natural scene. For

Alberti, the laws of form were also the laws of nature. They lay in perspective, "the means by which we arrive at proportion," providing that harmony of parts which was the Renaissance ideal of beauty. Nature was an organism not hostile to man but akin to him, a fresh idea which was to open up new worlds.

If, with the use of scientific perspective, recorded landscapes can successfully create an impression of the real thing, when this achievement is accompanied by the new secularization of art and a passionate interest in antiquity, as it was in the Renaissance, extraordinary visions of life are possible, as in the masterpiece of Perugino in the chapterhouse of Sta. Maria Maddalena de' Pazzi, in which the Umbrian landscape expresses the mood of the whole picture. "The past is fascinating because it is the one free place for our imagination." The *rinascimento*, in reviving the classical past, opened up a new range of feeling in man. Admirers of Petrarch, who represented the new humanism, had an unlimited enthusiasm for classical architecture, sculpture, and drawing (the last-named being encouraged as an aid in the study of human anatomy). Influenced by Pollaiuolo's interest in the human body and topographical landscapes, Botticelli embarked on the first monumental mythological pictures (the *Primavera* and the *Birth of Venus*). Here was a step toward Weltanschauung, with its double meaning (philosophy and world view or outlook), establishing a bridge between looking and the life of the mind. The comprehension of landscape is indeed more than pure vision. In this respect, Friedlander makes the point that *land* is the thing in itself, while *landscape* is the phenomenon. You may, like the farmer, know the land, but not always the landscape. It may take the artist to provide this knowledge. The artist devises a means of recording accurately what he sees. Alberti, for example, in an important work on cartography, anticipates the first accurate map making, which is finally achieved by Mercator a hundred years after Alberti's death. Leonardo and Dürer followed Alberti's lead and became surveying cartographers.[8] But Alberti's interest in the "phenomenon" goes much further. Dürer may have made the first modern watercolor of a town (a view of Innsbruck, now in the Albertina[9]) but Alberti was the first to define the street as an architectural unity and the square as a structural entity. He also stressed the visual quality of roads. All this stems from the Renaissance preoccupation with the harmony of parts and the idea of

PROSPETTIVA. In her right hand she holds a book by John Peckham, archbishop of Canterbury, called *Perspectiva Communis*; in her left an astrolabe.

proportion achieved by perspective. Perspective appears as the tenth liberal art on Pollaiuolo's tomb of Sixtus IV in the Grotte Vaticane, Rome, in the form of a beautiful girl holding a book on natural perspective in one hand and an astrolabe in the other. Her name is Prospettiva.[10]

The Topographers

"Be a plain topographer if you possibly can," said Ruskin in *Modern Painters* (1856). "If Nature meant you to be anything else she will force you to it." This was long after topographical painting had become a form of art in its own right. The golden age of the landscapist—"the cunning painter, limning a landscape"—was the seventeenth century. Everybody who was anybody acquired paintings of scenery. Go to Peter the Great's restored little Trianon "Monplaisir" at Peterhof and see copies of the Dutch landscapes he acquired when in Holland, learning the secrets of her shipbuilding industry. Even before the proliferation of easel-painted views, a recognizable *local* background to religious or historical pictures had become common and the artist had been forced to look more closely at nature, even though the finished product was not produced *en plein air*.[11] Aerial perspective (a device credited to Leonardo), which showed the far distance to be hazy rather than minutely detailed like the foreground (as in a van Ecyk) gave further verisimilitude to the painted image.

One did not ask a Vermeer or a Brueghel to record scenes on the Grand Tour, but an English milord, nonetheless, would sometimes employ a lesser topographical or view painter to travel with his suite through Europe. One of these was the draughtsman and engraver Wenceslaus Hollar, born in Prague, whom the earl of Arundel invited in 1636 to commemorate a journey to Vienna. Most of Hollar's engravings and wash drawings, like those by other seventeenth- and eighteenth-century view painters, were of scenes in the cities or of panoramic views of them from across a river. The Dutch made such scenes, including the streetscape, familiar, just as they had satisfied the rising bourgeoisie's desire for seascapes and allegorical paintings of the seasons. The Venetians, not to be outdone, had their Canaletto, his nephew Bellotto, and the Guardi family, whose works were purchased by visiting aristocrats and ambassadors long before tourism made the Grand Canal and the Rialto Bridge familiar to everyone. And although the limitations of the painter's technique inevitably resulted in distortions (variations in the apparent height of the campanile in Venice being as numerous as those who painted it), a landscape was as well lighted in the distance as in the foreground (such as one could find in Bellotto's views of Dresden, Vienna, and Warsaw), and in which all the trees were distinguishable, was considered an infallible *aide-memoire*; today it is once more sought after as a work of art in its own right. Thus painters influenced the rationalist's view of nature, just as the camera, with its own revelations and distortions, has come to influence ours.

Like the poet Cowper in *The Task*, one might enjoy *veduti* as substitutes for travel:

> None more admires—the painter's magic skill,
> Who shows me that which I shall never see,
> Conveys a distant country into mine,
> And throws Italian light on English walls.

The Dutch landscape, which we instantly recognize from paintings when first we see its limitless skies and distant rainshowers, was considered worthy of painting "without trimmings or accessories" after 1600, partly, according to Fried-

THE NATURAL BRIDGE BECOMES A FAVORITE THEME OF ARTISTS. This one is an early example from the pen of Gian-Francesco Barbieri (called Guercino because of his squint) (1591–1666). Such unusual forms were also painted by Filipo Neopolitano, whose seascapes influenced the French painter Claude Lorraine. Claude returned again and again to memories of the Bay of Naples for his famous landscapes. Bizarre forms of trees and rocks were favored by the late Mannerists by whom Claude was also influenced in his earlier works. Others who delighted in *outré* geological forms were Gaspard Dughet (called Dughet-Poussin after his more famous brother-in-law), Salvator Rosa, and Sebastiano Ricci. (American painters also cast their eyes on the natural bridge: see Thomas Cole's *Manhood* in his series *The Voyage of Life*.)

lander, because the country had been bitterly fought for and its independence guaranteed by the 1620s. Van Goyen, Cuyp, Rubens, Rembrandt, and countless others painted the landscapes of home, while French landscape painting seemed to bloom on Italian soil. Later, of course, all nations were to enshrine local scenery. Gainsborough remarked that England's fields and hedges "lent gentility" to simple nature, while Constable made famous the mills and byways of Suffolk, showing that the works of man were everywhere compatible with the countryside before the peasant folkways began to disappear in the age of steam and iron.[12]

Constable's love of rustic scenery was matched by the elemental simplicity of expression which Wordsworth brought to the scenes of his own boyhood. The most influential nature poet of the Western world (excluding possibly Virgil) uses landscape as a bridge to the understanding of life and human values. And unlike John Clare's Northhamptonshire, the Lake District has never been the same since.

Every poet since Petrarch has sung of nature in one way or another, although with some the acknowledgement has only been the briefest nod. The climbing of Mont Ventoux (a peak of 6,427 feet) in 1336, recorded in Petrarch's letter to Dionisio Roberti of Borgo San Sepolcro, reveals the mountains in a new perspective: behind the human scene but also above, another manifestation of God's power. Yet Petrarch is not primarily a nature poet, and some of those who were later called that, like Thompson and Dyer, were using painterly images; their scenery is all broken rocks and rushing skies. Dyer sings a paean to the painter Claude Lorrain, who idealized nature for the British landscape gardener, while Thompson in *The Castle of Indolence* admires

> Whate'er *Lorrain* light-touchd with softening Hue,
> Or savage *Rosa* dashed, or learned *Poussin* drew.

There is none of this bravura in Wordsworth—quite the opposite. He prefers the sublime to the picturesque, and his images, although often dramatic, are based on his own pastoral observations.

Unlike the poet Gray (1716–71), who wrote of mountains, "None of these monstrous creatures of God know how to join so much beauty with so much horror," and carried a Claude glass on his travels, Wordsworth knew the connection of man with the world:

> . . . he, who feels contempt
> For any living thing, hath faculties
> Which he has never used.

In Wordsworth's day poets were becoming familiar with the world of science and had not rejected it, as so many were to do in a later "art for art's sake" generation.

Wordsworth evidenced familiarity with many aspects of geology in his *Guide to the Lakes*, first published in 1810. He knew rather more about forest trees and the native flora, advising landowners on what and what not to plant on their estates. He had his eye on the "Improvers," whose efforts to increase the value of their properties did not always result in the betterment of the land. Yet, as might be expected, his approach is quite different from that of the scientist. He describes the forms of mountains briefly, but lingers over their surfaces and colors, as well as their natural coverings. (It will be remembered that had he not chosen poetry, Wordsworth considered himself endowed by nature to pursue two other callings, those of landscape gardener and critic of paintings.) Too, he is fascinated by the habitations of man and by domestic incidents, as well as bucolic scenery. He gives a great deal of thought to the appearance of lakes—they are best when not resembling rivers and they should not be too large (perhaps a shade of Lake District chauvinism appears when the poet calls Loch Lomond monotonous in its expanse).[13] It is more important for lakes to be numerous and their shores to be indented. By these standards his own lakes qualify, while the American and Asiatic lakes have "the blankness of a sea-prospect without the grandeur and accompanying sense of power."

As the apostle of Natural Beauty, Wordsworth anticipates much of the modern conservationist's beliefs. Alien species of plants he decries as also the work of the Improvers. Intrusions and discordant objects create harsh contrasts in a landscape of fine gradations. Houses or mansions suited to a mountainous region should be "not obvious, not obtrusive, but retired." He does not favor houses being painted white, citing a case in which a white house reduced the apparent size of a mountain.

If thou art one
On fire with thy impatience to become
An inmate of these mountains,—if, disturbed

By beautiful conceptions, thou hast hewn
Out of the quiet rock the elements
Of thy trim Mansion destined soon to blaze
In snow-white splendour,—think again; and . . . leave
Thy fragments to the bramble and the rose.

["Inscription with a Slate Pencil upon a Stone"]

Wordsworth is intensely aware of the effects of landscape on the eye, much more than many another poet whose visual images are often borrowed from literary sources. It is this kind of borrowing that caused John Clare to refer deprecatingly to Keat's "Grecian fripperies."

The lakes ought to be considered "a sort of national property," Wordsworth maintained. As early as 1755, according to one of Wordsworth's biographers, an Oxford don had published his "Descriptive Poem Addressed to Two Ladies at their Return from Viewing the Mines near Whitehaven," in which, using fluent octosyllabic verse, "he praises with magnificent impartiality the triumphant advance of commercial enterprise and the natural beauty of Keswick, Skiddaw and Lodore." By the time Wordsworth was walking the country this attitude was changing; in 1844 he was moved to protest the coming of the Kendall and Windermere Railway:

Speak, pressing winds; ye torrents with your strong
And constant voice, protest against the wrong.

In a letter to the *Morning Post* he points out that other railways already bring tourists to an acceptable distance and that the desire for natural scenery is new, and to be fulfilled slowly by "a gradual process of culture." Not by rushing through it on a railway!

Wordsworth made the Lake District, already a tourist resort, into what we would call today an object of cultural tourism. He and his sister Dorothy created a landscape of the mind, as those who themselves sought out the scenes of his poetry soon discovered. Like painters, poets infuse their landscapes with values which transform the actual picture seen.[14]

When the *Guide to the Lakes* appeared again, in 1842, sections on geology and botany were added by the publishers, as if to emphasize the growing public interest in the natural sciences. Nowadays, when presumably we know much that there is to be known about lavas, tuffs, and agglomerates of the Ordovician Borrowdale Volcanic Series, and the older grits, flagstones, shales, and mudstones of the Skiddaw Slate Series, we look back to Wordsworth not only for his topographical evocations but for the first principles of landscape conservation to be laid down by an Englishman. His idea of the Lake District as national property is as important a milestone for the parks movement as the call made in 1844 by another poet, William Cullen Bryant, for an urban park in New York City, a proposal that eventually led to the creation of Central Park as we know it today.

John Ruskin, another long-term resident of the Lake District (he spent the last thirty years of his life there, having first visited Keswick with his parents at the age of five), was also an opponent of railways. Instead of building them, he thought, "we should have built churches and houses of beauty." He was convinced of "the certainty of the deterioration of the moral character in the inhabitants of every district penetrated by the railway."[15] The old order of society appealed to him and he projected it into his models for a new English social life. Like William Morris, he looked on the medieval world of guilds and the Gothic spirit, handcrafting, and closeness to nature as ideals for a society which had created the dark and noisy industrial town. Architecture depended on painting, he taught, and he found "a look of mountain brotherhood between the cathedral and the alp."

In Ruskin's day the mountains had already become the temples of the educated middle classes, and nature worship was frequently reflected in painting as well as poetry. Poets like Southey and Coleridge are associated with the Lake District, but its painters are less well known, with the exception of J. M. W. Turner, whom Ruskin had helped to launch. They include Francis Towne, who painted there in the 1780s, Thomas Girtin, Daniel Gardner, and Julius Caesar Ibbetson, who sold his landscapes to wealthy tourists in the first decade of the nineteenth century.

View of Loch Lomond by the Reverend William Gilpin (1724–1804), a celebrator of natural scenery who is known as the father of the picturesque. He was the model for the satirical poem "Dr. Syntax."

New Images of Landscape

If the Renaissance made possible realistic approximations of what the eye sees, the nineteenth century, avid for new experiences, transformed the art of painting by concentrating on further exploitation of technique, first in color and then in form. It remained for the present century to attempt to abstract content from painting, an approach now in its turn passing into limbo.

Wordsworth's contemporaries, Constable and Turner, were notable pioneers, the former, according to Christopher Hussey, showing the public how to appreciate landscape "through the juxtaposition of tints." He so impressed the French at the 1824 "Salon des Anglais" that even they have agreed that his influence may have led eventually toward Impressionism; they give credit as well to Turner, whose passion for color produced violent illusions of light in sea and sky. It was in this period just as possible to see a landscape as "a juxtaposition of tints" as it was at the end of the century to see the clothed bones of Mont Sainte-Victoire through Cézanne's eyes. Earlier, the Reverend William Gilpin (1724–1804), whose books were said to have created "a new class of travels," could write of a distant mountainside and say of its hues, "they seem to be a sort of floating silky colors—always in motion—always in harmony—and playing with a thousand changeable varieties into each other." Gilpin was an excellent topographical painter and had trained himself to see the essence of things, but a later critic regretted the passing of "the noble, fine prospect" that Impressionism's fleeting glance had made unfashionable, noting how her contemporaries placed "a terrible over-importance on the act of vision." Color and light are variable, and "we may be disappointed when the woods, which we had seen as vague, moss-like blue before the sun had overtopped the hills, become at mid-day a mere vast lettuce-bed."[16]

If France is considered the key to much that is significant in modern painting, especially for the influence of what is generally called the School of Paris, it should be remembered that "the changeover from composed landscape to spontaneous studies after nature took place within the institutional framework" and was not, as is generally supposed, an act of rebellion on the part of a few progressives.[17] The famous French Academy did not ignore landscape, but included it as part of the Prix de Rome as early as 1817. In 1800 Valenciennes had published his work on perspective and landscape, claiming that it was a branch of art in its own right. Valenciennes avowed that he had visited and studied "almost all the gardens in the vicinity of Rome and Paris." In his *Theorie de Paysage* (1818) Deperthes, a pupil of Valenciennes, defined the *style champêtre* as

. . . an expanse of country dominated by an area of sky and seen in the light that falls on it at the exact moment when the painter sets out to capture the scene.[18]

Landscape painting gradually took precedence over historical painting; this movement coincides with the cutting off of visual art from science and also from poetry. Like the ornamental art of the East, landscape became the perfect subject matter for the art-for-art's-sake movement, since land as an object had no demands to make on the intellect, merely on the senses. Today, there is even a reaction against the anti-humanism of abstract and Surrealist art. The landscape is again peopled with figures and the prospect ennobled by a new understanding of nature's ways. The belief that man must live with the landscape as well as in it should enable us to see it differently and with a stronger poetic sensibility than ever before. Like Alberti we are learning to draw everything from nature, in both senses of the word.

The much-discussed influence of photography on our impressions of the world has had a one-sided effect. Superb from a scientific point of view for recording either microorganisms, moisture content and flow, indications of pollution, population density, or large sections of the earth's surface from many miles in space, the camera's scope is seemingly unlimited. When the Daguerreotype was first invented, Daguerre proudly announced in his prospectus that he was now able "to portray Nature without the aid of an artist." But the nonselective character of the device left something to be desired that only the artist could provide. As the artists were apt to say, "Not what actually exists, but only what can be seen to exist, may legitimately become the subject of art." Some of them used the camera in their work; its appearance is said to have led to Naturalism. On the other hand, the decline of good drawing has been attributed to it. The great colorist Delacroix, for instance, is known to have used the camera extensively. The camera reveals nature's secrets, he thought, and "if a man of genius uses the Daguerreotype as it should be used, he will elevate [his art] to a height hitherto unknown." Recent technology has produced infrared photography and other novelties which overdramatize landscapes. If the advances in technique can be said to have influenced our way of looking at scenery, that influence may be manifested by increased boredom with what *is*, as opposed to what the camera can make us see. Modern man's saturation with images is another matter. Movie and television cameras, transmitting countless recorded pictures and signs, are only agents of powerful interests who use them either for their own ends or for the public good.

Two British painters in particular have helped the cause of natural and man-made scenes in our time. Paul Nash was unique among English modern painters in depicting the most minute details of natural objects, along with a command of the sweep of sky over broad plains, seascapes, and country parks. For the former interest he was called a Surrealist, but although his house in Hampstead was crammed with "found objects" mostly given him by the postman and other friends and admirers, and in spite of the remarkable grotto he had made in the garden (which appears in some of his paintings), he did not give himself a label, being a master of every element in his compositions and never ceasing to celebrate the beauties of the English landscape. It was my privilege in the 1930s to know well an artist who could paint and write so sensitively of the natural world. He died all too soon for the cause of the preservation of Britain's natural beauty.

It is a rare thing for a modern painter to be as concerned as John Piper with his object of study. Sir John Betjeman has remarked that abstract painting was an insufficient outlet for Piper, who became an excellent topographical writer as well as an easel painter and designer of scenery. Accepting the premise that one can never love art until one loves what it mirrors better, Piper has explored caves and waterfalls and has asked himself about the purpose and propriety of "Georgian shop-fronts, Gothick country houses and the Victorian facades of public houses, as well as of the life that goes on inside and behind these."[19]

Piper coined the term "pleasing decay." "The planner might find it sensible," he wrote, "to retain the tower of a redundant church, and the fabric of a non-conformist chapel as visual points of interest in one new development scheme, a decayed warehouse or a terrace of houses of decayed charm in another. These in fact have a visual point, not only for their own sakes but for the sake of relief and contrast." He quotes Henry James (from *English Hours*, 1905) on the beauty of

A Paul Nash watercolor, *Bridge over the Dyke* (1924).

moss-grown crumbling churches "where the wild flowers were a cornice and the sailing clouds a roof." He finds that Ruskin and Cotman and William Morris articulated a similar understanding of man's relation to nature.

At the same time, Piper finds fault with those restoration and conservation measures which tend to give buildings a "dated" look (dating from the time of the restoration, that is), one that anyone who has been to Carcassonne, that nineteenth-century medieval "bourg," will recognize. Yet he thinks that to leave a

PLEASING DECAY. John Piper's sketch of the facade of St. Marie's Grange, home of neo-medieval architect Augustus Welby Pugin. The Grange was built in 1835 near Salisbury in Wiltshire. It is, according to Piper, "the grandfather of suburban Gothic."

building or a town alone and let it fall to pieces, which is the way we would see Carcassonne today if Viollet-le-Duc had not engaged in its wholesale reconstruction, is not a very satisfactory solution. Perform the act with sensibility is Piper's advice, and *ignore fashion*, which is always conditioned by the guide books. People tend to talk about restorations as "tasteful" when they are done and as "acts of vandalism" fifty years later. The international preservation movement has recently tried to obviate this unfortunate result by urging only the most necessary conservation measures and the retention of additions to historic buildings made later in their lives. Piper anticipated this by advising would-be restorers to "regard the present state of the building as, possibly, virtuous in itself." Above all, he urged, rely on the eyes.

Diseases of stone, tree roots, damp—all the elements of decay, pleasing or not—are nature's way of bringing back everything into her arms, sooner or later. Still one must do something about stopping the rot. We have new chemicals and better means of doing so than when Piper wrote; in fact, we can arrest decay at almost any stage, making its pleasure permanent. But he puts his finger on a modern problem when he says that archaeologists have taken over from artists. Rome has become "a place of interest" rather than "a place of beauty."

Piper tells us to look at a building three times before pulling it down; first, to be sure that it has no virtues that will be sadly missed; second, to see that it will not be missed as an enrichment to its present surroundings; and third, to estimate whether or not it may form a useful focal point, either by consonance or contrast, in future surroundings. We are armed today with protective inventories and other measures for scheduling preservation of the manmade environment, yet the eye of the painter may yet see deeper into the needs and obligations of society in maintaining a cultural fabric for the future than we are apt to acknowledge.

Novel Landscapes

It is unusual for novels of any period not to incorporate descriptions of landscape. Indeed, from at least the time of Sir Walter Scott, novelists have deemed evocation of setting a central part of their art, and many of the landscapes we find most familiar we know from literature.

It may be instructive to note here a few writers who have affected our way of seeing natural and man-made scenes by bringing to our attention aspects of them that might otherwise never have been revealed.

> This magic prose not only evokes for us the river and its shore, the forests and their trees, but it does so by giving us, at one and the same time, the most minute details and the sense of the whole.[20]

It is quite possible, I believe, to relate the man-made forms we see around us to the literature of the period in which they have been created. Thus the curvilinear street plan, now so popular in American suburbs, can first be found around New York during the period of the post-Romantic movement. Poe and Melville in that day set the stage for the picturesque suburbs and parks created by Alexander Jackson Davis and Andrew Jackson Downing. Similarly, it would be fascinating (although probably depressing) to trace in the anarchy and confusion of much American postwar writing some relationship to the faceless, synthetic mass building now prevalent in any city of the United States. But it may be more important, and certainly less open to error, to analyze a more direct relationship—that of the writer to his immediate material and his ideas about the present, ideas which still have currency. One who believes in tradition at all must be firmly convinced of this. On how many bookshelves will one find Melville's *Pierre*—yet this novel poses once and for all the dualism of city and country life. Who now reads the novels of Rebecca Harding Davis, one of the earliest writers on the effects of industrialism, or those of Constance Fenimore Woolson, whose observations of the Cleveland Flats in the 1870s are perhaps the first to describe the "blue barrels" of the oil men who ushered in our present age of power.

Literary perception of form is revealed by various means. Usually the form is background and may be just a needed stage prop, a way of giving the characters "position" in space and time. Very often it is direct, as in Balzac, who is possibly the greatest master of the urban scene. His Paris is the mysterious multicelled city Paris really is, the Paris equally of garret and salon, and his imagery in describing it serves to heighten all our feelings. Who else would think of describing a northern city in its relation to the sun, "setting fire to its golden crosses," or comparing it with a giant lobster, its thousand claws atremble? By contrast, the Paris of Flaubert is seen in fragments, through the eyes of his novels' protagonists; scenes of the city are of a single instant and have no intrinsic life of their own.[21] Dickens uses a very personal method of making his characters' houses take on the attributes of their inhabitants; each seems perfectly suited to the other. Dickens, unlike Balzac, seldom brings to life a whole city as a single, living artifact. His description of Coketown occupies but a paragraph in *Hard Times:*

> It was a town of red brick, or of brick that would have been red if the smoke and ashes had allowed it; but as matters stood it was a town of unnatural red and black like the painted face of a savage. It was a town of machinery and tall chimneys, out of which interminable serpents of smoke trailed themselves for ever and ever, and never got uncoiled. It has a black canal in it, and a river that ran purple with ill-smelling dye, and vast piles of building full of windows where there was a rattling and a trembling all day long, and where the piston of the steam-engine worked monotonously up and down like the head of an elephant in a state of melancholy madness. It contained several large streets all very like one another, and many small streets still more like one another, inhabited by people equally like one another, who all went in and out at the same hours, with the same sound upon the same pavements, to do the same work, and to whom every day was the same as yesterday and tomorrow, and every year the counterpart of the last and the next.[22]

If we follow Dickens to New York, we will find that he, like Matthew Arnold, is as much interested in our institutions as in the physical urban scene. He cleverly makes Broadway come alive in terms of the people on its sidewalks, but like so many others after him he is appalled by the disparity between American ideals and their absence in the materialism of everyday life. This blinds him to much that is scenically rewarding. One would never know from reading *American Notes* that New York in that day had a seat of government which is still the handsomest building in the city or a residential district like leafy Hudson Square, which Mrs.

Trollope found "both fashionable and beautiful." There is a hilarious description in *Martin Chuzzlewit* of a New York boardinghouse—an institution now completely vanished from the American scene—and a scarifying one of a fashionable home in which a visitor is treated with utmost courtesy until it is discovered that he has arrived in New York as a steerage passenger, at which revelation he is asked to leave! So, even apart from his attacks on American newspapers, his savage description of the Congress, and his constant references to the American habit of chewing and spitting tobacco ("Washington may be called the headquarters of tobacco-tinctured saliva"), it is no wonder that Dickens was the target of outraged American criticism. His picture is highly colored and incomplete.

I should like to contrast Dickens's approach to the city with that of Ruskin, who reputedly would not visit this country—because it had no castles! Ruskin can still dazzle with his prose, and there would probably be little question that his account of the approach and entrance to Saint Mark's Square is the most compelling and blazing urban description in all English literature. I have no doubt that it can still be very moving, with its wild symbolism and ingenious juxtaposition of English crows with Venetian doves. To Ruskin the cathedral was a vision out of the earth; his clever preparation of the reader only makes the ensuing description more splendid. Unlike Dickens, however, Ruskin wanted to reform the world through art. He believed that if people could feel about art as he did, their lives would be as beautiful as Tintoretto's religious scenes. This led him to many more descriptive excursions than Dickens ever had to take, and people followed him by building in the style he advocated. Ruskinian Gothic became as popular in America as in England. The city hall in New Haven is one of the first examples built here. Its timid and now faded polychromy is but a faint echo of Venetian or Lombard architecture. Perhaps fortunately, the style did not last very long: Ruskin outlived it. He was appalled by what he saw, even though he had personally directed the building of the "gothic" Oxford Museum. He felt that the Renaissance should be abjured. But ultimately he knew that he had failed. All Gothic revival predilections had vanished by the 1890s. Of these two great Victorians there is no question that Dickens had improved the city more—and people's lives—without prescribing a single architectural remedy.

In a country like the United States, which has drawn so largely on experience in its literature, writers' native habitats have usually been more than adequately portrayed (think of Whitman or Hart Crane). Curiously, however, the more perceptive writers, at least as far as the city is concerned, are those in whom acquired knowledge rather than experience alone has been specially brought to bear. Henry James had made a study of painting with the help of Charles Eliot Norton and had met Ruskin, Rossetti, and Morris before he could charm us in *The Wings of the Dove* with these painterly terms:

> Venice glowed and plashed and called and chimed again; the air was like a clap of hands, and the scattered pinks, yellows, blues, sea-greens, were like a hanging out of vivid stuffs, a laying-down of fine carpets.[23]

With James—and especially in *The American Scene*—we reach the peak of insight into the American city, its bad as well as good aspects. That he could see the beauties at a time when the American public was being smothered in ugliness with the work of Frank Norris, Upton Sinclair, and Lincoln Steffens is something to be grateful for. If New York personified to him a woman of the streets, he could nevertheless find in Washington a more wonderful symbolism, something that other writers had been unable to do. To achieve this extraordinary reciprocity between writer and physical scene, James uses some special devices—that of making buildings talk to each other, for instance, recalling their purpose and their past, or the device of sudden contrast, so that one is startled in a description of a New England village by the intrusion of a reference to Spain. All this makes us see the view in deep perspective or in a new light. Washington, for example, is a garden:

> . . . the perpetual perspectives, the converging, radiating avenues, the frequent circles and crossways, where all that was wanted for full illusion was that the bronze generals and admirals, on their named pedestals, should have been great garden-gods, mossy mythological marble. This would have been the perfect note; the long vistas yearned for it, and the golden chequers

scattered through the gaps of the high arches waited for some bending nymph or some armless Hermes to pick them up.[24]

The allusion is all the more piquant when one realizes that the planner of Washington, Pierre L'Enfant, grew up in the gardens of Versailles, where his father was a painter to the court.

But in Washington it is the architectural focal point of the composition that James experiences so vividly, and he has ingeniously masked the real point by dwelling on the trivialities of gossip and rumor that pervade the capital today as then.

Listen to James talking of the house of the Congress, on its acropolis height, which "rakes" the view, "as it rakes the continent, to a much more sweeping purpose." You are somehow possessed of *all* the American scene, he says, as you tread the marble steps, which are "the complement of the vast democratic lap." He talks of the "immeasurable schemes" of which the building consciously remains the center. He sees a trio of Indian braves, their pockets full of photographs and cigarettes. The Indians "seemed just then and there, for a mind fed betimes on the Leatherstocking Tales, to project as in a flash an image in itself immense, but foreshortened and simplified—reducing to a single smooth stride the bloody footsteps of time. One rubbed one's eyes, but there, at its highest polish, shining in the beautiful day, was the brazen face of history, and there, all about one, immaculate, the printless pavements of the State."

James proposed no utopias, no "might-have-beens" such as we find in Vitruvius's description of the plan of Dinocrates, no prescription like Aristotle's for laying out a city. (If we find so few philosophers preoccupied with the total form, why indeed should we expect our literary mandarins to offer us this sort of vision?) Perceptive as always, he observed, for instance, that the true American square was indoors, not outdoors as in Italy, and could be found in the lobby of the big city hotel; and that the country club was "the apotheosis of the family in America." He is full of insights of this kind and talk about the future, if not the solution for it (which so preoccupied his English neighbor and pupil, H. G. Wells). Naturally, in a country which has had more utopian and sectarian com-

A VIEW WITH MUSICAL AND LITERARY ASSOCIATIONS. The Stockbridge Bowl and Monument Mountain seen from one of the entrances to Tanglewood. Although they might not recognize the scene in its winter clothing, over six million outdoor concertgoers may have enjoyed it in July and August up to this time. Fanny Kemble admired the sunsets from here. Nearby, along the road, stood the house of Nathaniel Hawthorne (which has been reconstructed), where he came to live just after finishing *The Scarlet Letter*. Hawthorne called Monument Mountain, in its autumn garb, "the headless Sphinx wrapped in a Persian shawl." In one of its caves he met Herman Melville for the first time when the two were taking shelter from a thunderstorm.

munities than any other, we expect to find literary utopias, but they are not especially revealing—they are, for example, much less specifically drawn than Plato's Atlantis—of notions of urban form. One of the very best is William Dean Howells's Altruria, described in his two novels of social criticism, in which he places the utopia on another continent to point up its contrasts with turn-of-the-century America.[25]

Howells and James wrote of a period in which the city was truly a center of culture, but James's shrewd remarks about the country club portended the immediate future: there would soon be no inhabitants for the mansions on Fifth Avenue. People were moving away.

The city was being destroyed—by writers as much as by anyone.

> The view up the river was magnificent, quite the finest which the city had to offer; but it was ruined by a hideous gas-tank, placed squarely in the middle of it. And this, again, was not inappropriate—it was typical of all the ways of the city. It was a city which had grown up by accident, with nobody to care about it or to help it; it was huge and ungainly, crude, uncomfortable, and grotesque. There was nowhere in it a beautiful sight upon which a man could rest his eyes, without having them tortured by something ugly near by. At the foot of the slope of the River Drive ran a hideous freight-railroad; and across the river the beautiful Palisades were being blown to pieces to make paving stone—and meantime were covered with advertisements of land-companies. And if there was a beautiful building, there was sure to be a tobacco advertisement beside it; if there was a beautiful avenue, there were trucks and overworked horses toiling in the harness; if there was a beautiful park, it was filled with wretched, outcast men. Nowhere was any order or system—everything was struggling for itself, and jarring and clashing with everything else; and this broke the spell of power which the Titan city would otherwise have produced. It seemed like a monstrous heap of wasted energies; a mountain in perpetual labour, and producing an endless series of abortions. The men and women in it were wearing themselves out with toil; but there was a spell laid upon them, so that, struggle as they might, they accomplished nothing.[26]

Fortunately, this upper West Side vista would be improved—by Robert Moses, with funds from the federal government—but the city as a whole was to become much worse than Sinclair saw it. And gradually writers themselves began to find in it nothing but ugliness and evil.

The slum had been explored—so thoroughly that before long something was going to be done about it—but a new form of community had meanwhile sprung up: the American suburb. Among the most significant writers of the decade of the twenties, when first real suburbs came into being, was Sinclair Lewis. His descriptions in *Dodsworth*—"here was everything he had gone abroad to seek"—are so accurate and revealing that it will be difficult ever to surpass them.

Writers questioned the virtues of the small town, but in the main they wrote of it constantly and nostalgically—Carol Kennicot begins by hating Gopher Prairie, but she returns to it willingly in the end. Russell Lynes has examined this nostalgia, so notable in Thomas Wolfe and others. He points out that writers who came to the big city shunned it in their work and dwelt nostalgically on the small towns of their origin.[27] A few, like John O'Hara, were realistic about the American town, no longer the center of rural virtue, but American writers on the whole invested it with a macabre romanticism, Faulkner among them. For these writers, the small town, with all its faults, was still the center, long after the illusion that it would be the focus of American life had been dispelled. Taking their cues from Spengler and Lewis Mumford, they speculated pessimistically on what they saw as the inevitable decline of the American city. Other writers, too, and especially poets, have anticipated the death agony of the city. Even Goethe in 1811 sighs:

> The tallest houses crack,
> Whole cities fall;
> And do you think perhaps
> This cob wall of my heart,
> Mere straw and clay and gravel,
> Will not collapse?
>
> ["Sicilian Song"]

But this was a love song, its city a plaything of the heart. It is our own generation which hopes for nothing but the city's fall. We see in the cult of Thoreau and in a spate of nature writing in the thirties and forties a turning away from the city and all that it stands for—or we see the city used as a setting for such sin-burdened tragedies as *Studs Lonigan* and *Butterfield 8*.

The fifties saw a revival of interest in the city and a curious realization in a very few writers of what the city in our time is likely to be, a new revelation of its total form. The poems of Lawrence Ferlinghetti and the novels of certain men like Jack Kerouac and after him Tom Wolfe[28] evidenced a sense of the modern city not to be found in the works of previous decades. These writers discovered another dimension to American living—a secondary landscape, as Brinckerhoff Jackson put it—and were in tune with the extension of the city to the dimensions of the continent. Instead of rejecting the city, they carried it comfortably with them wherever they went—and, like our modern lines of communication, they went far. Accepting time and motion, accepting the city as a natural phenomenon alternately exhilarating and bewildering, they made us look at the city in a new way, much as Dickens made people look at London. Kerouac's description of Denver may not be the Denver you and I know, but it certainly existed, with its thousands of high school youths, trailer owners, cops, forlorn mistresses, and hot dog stand proprietors—in many ways the modern equivalent of a Dickensian cast of characters.

Here is a view of the Mississippi from Kerouac's *On the Road:*

> On rails we leaned and looked at the great brown father of waters rolling down from mid-America like the torrent of broken souls—bearing Montana logs and Dakota muds and Iowa vales and things that had drowned in Three Forks, where the secret began in ice.[29]

The road is where all the excitement is. "It's the world!" shouts the hero, who gets his kicks from stealing expensive cars and driving them from city to city at 110 miles an hour. The scenery is all clutter—billboards and huts and neon lights and automotive sales yards—a giant urban region inherited by this generation from its fathers'. Kerouac's is a world of 40,000 trailers in the uranium country, of the junk heaps of New Jersey, of a youth disgusted with suburbia and even with bohemia, which fascinated the writers of Scott Fitzgerald's era. The new world set forth in fiction like Kerouac's is a kind of outer bohemia, but is quite real, despite its many unpleasant overtones. It happens to illuminate more scholarly examinations of the great urban regions of America, which are based on the spines of our highway system, in a quite remarkable way. It is the literature of a more fluid society, and its greatest virtues are that it is naive rather than cynical and is based less on hatred than on curiosity.

It is curiosity, after all, which will enable the writer to reveal those facets of the environment which have been obscured in recent years. Now that we have begun to redevelop the run-down parts of our communities and set up planning controls for highways and industry far out into the rural areas, we need such raking glances, if only as a corrective to an approach to our surroundings based on expediency or efficiency, which leaves no room for poetry, art, or atmosphere, and leads only to creations without soul.

Since the departure of the Beat Generation, modern fiction has added little to our knowledge of the physical world. The best writing has been concerned with the devastation of war, ethnic determination, and dynamic social change. This is also true of stage dramas. One looks outside literature nowadays for signs of a deeper appreciation of landscape. "Protest against the wrong" (the rape of the environment) has become the prerogative of a new generation of young people. They may not all be able to write well, but they will not remain silent. It is encouraging today to know that the curiosity of youth leads not merely to escapism but increasingly to an appreciation of the landscape through such outdoor activities as hiking, backpacking, bicycling, and exploration of the wild. Such activities have given countless young people memorable experience of natural beauty and excellent opportunities to understand the landscape in both macrocosm and microcosm.

One cannot be so sanguine about the role of the visual artist. He who has been so important in the past has developed ambivalent attitudes. On the one hand, as we have seen, art records changing perceptions of landscape; on the other, art influences landscape changes itself. If Albert Bierstadt's dramatic landscape paintings of the west, together with Matthew Brady's photographs, contributed to the formation of national parks, what of the countless images of our civilization as a wasteland and *their* influence? Even the best of America's twentieth-century "academic" artists—Edward Hopper, for instance—have imbued their landscapes with a melancholy *angst*, while certain of the more distinguished photographers have changed the picture of the American west to one of sparse austerity. When James Fenimore Cooper observed that in the United States views were of sufficient extent "to conceal the want of finish in the details," he was not influenced by photography; it is interesting to hear, however, that modern American photographers "give a picture of the land that is often harsh, always spacious, and whose lines are sharp and contrasts brilliant . . . sinuous desert ridges, serrated rocks."[24] It seems likely that this ubiquitous medium, dispersed through millions of magazine and newspaper images, may have given today's citizen a most specialized idea of his landscapes—a vaguely hostile world, untamed, a wastescape.

> The age demanded an image
> Of its accelerated grimace,
> Something for the modern stage,
> Not, at any rate, an Attic grace.
>
> [Ezra Pound, "Ode pour l'Election de son Sepulchre,"
> *Hugh Selwyn Mauberley*]

This passage may strike an echoing chord in many a modern mind, but it is easy and not very productive to talk about "a botched civilization," as Pound did, likening our world to "an old bitch gone in the teeth." Such facile denigrations will not produce clean air or better cities. Fortunately, there are enough people now celebrating landscape values in all sections of society to challenge the threats to their continued existence. That the new approach to life-giving elements of the environment can be assisted by the arts is manifest in what we have seen them able to accomplish. The new generation must ensure that art is not separated from life, or from that love of landscape that promises so much, like a gleam of light among the encircling clouds.

THE GARDEN

Privilege and Privacy

Man can enjoy the landscape in many ways: intimately, as does the outdoorsman, or remotely, as does the observer through a car window; he can lose himself in it, or appreciate its spectacle; he can plod up the hill, or rush down it on skis. And there are such specialized ways as the creation of personalized landscapes which give extraordinary opportunities for indulging the fancy. In these landscapes, too, man can wander at will or gaze from some vantage point, as did the esthetic Shogun Yoshimasa from his Silver Pavilion, watching for the moon to rise over the Kyoto hills.

When men use nature's materials, pliable yet often wayward and intransigent, to create landscapes in their own plot of land, the result may range from the sublime to the primitive, for there are both a fine art of gardens and a highly colored folk art. From the peony terraces of China to Prince Pückler's floral cornucopias at Muskau, from the hydraulic automata at Hellbrun to the shady groves of Persia, and from the labyrinths of the Tudors to the rationalist gardens of modern architecture, the variety of personal choices is extreme and always enlightening vis-à-vis the creators and clients. If you can tell a man's position in society by the house he builds, you can tell something else about him from his garden, in which the constraints are fewer and the opportunities for self-expression greater. Gardens are a luxury of the imagination, and the act of gardening self-indulgent but not necessarily elitist. Gardens can be light, amusing, or droll (topiary elephants), somber (funerary cypresses), practical (cottage gardens), refreshing (fountains and pools), or majestic (Versailles or Hampton Court). They likewise provide a welcome measure of eccentricity.

Privacy and leisure are essential to the gardening ethos. When Pliny the Younger visited his seaside villa near Rome, he advised a correspondent, "You should take the first opportunity yourself to leave the din, the futile bustle and

67

useless occupations of the city, and devote yourself to literature or to leisure."[1] Pliny had other villas; writing to Caninius Rufus he inquires, "I wonder how our darling Comum is looking, and your lovely house outside the town, with its colonnade where it is always springtime, and the shady plane trees, the stream with its sparkling greenish water flowing into the lake below, and the drive over the smooth firm turf . . . isn't it really time you handed over those tiresome petty duties to someone else and shut yourself up with your books in the complete peace and comfort of your retreat?"[2] Pliny described two of his own gardens, and these descriptions form the basis of our knowledge of the gardens of the ancients. We even know what he ate at his poolside, where the main dishes for dinner were set out on the edge of the basin, while the lighter ones floated in vessels shaped like birds or little boats. Chiding a guest who missed one such meal, Pliny described the menu: "It was all laid out, one lettuce each, three snails, two eggs, wheat-cake, and wine with honey chilled with snow . . . besides olives, beetroots, gherkins, onions, and any number of similar delicacies. You would have heard a comic play, a reader or singer, or all three if I felt generous. Instead you chose to go where you could have oysters, sow's innards, sea-urchins, and Spanish dancing-girls."

The villa garden is still with us, although few nowadays match the extent or intricacy of Pliny's, with their hot and cold baths, hippodromes, and colonnades. In the early Renaissance Alberti advised Florentine bankers and noblemen to build their retreats on the hills near the city: "A villa near town is extremely convenient for private business or public affairs."[3]

The Florentines had great difficulty recreating ancient gardens, but their emulation of the classical past was one of three main factors that would define the Renaissance artist's ethos, the others being the new science of perspective and the gradual secularization of art. No extensive gardens were left from Greek or Roman times. Literary sources consisted either of lists of plants grown or allegorical descriptions in Homer of Nymphaea or enchanted groves. Sculpture, fountains, basins, and masks there were in plenty, but most of them had been plundered from their original sites (although the site of Pliny's villa garden in Tuscany is supposed to have been identified from marble fragments scattered on the ground). The gardens of Pompeii had not been excavated, nor had several late

Roman villas elsewhere, including the great one at Piazza Armerina in Sicily. Thus, although they used plant materials that were known to the ancients—box and myrtle, yew and rosemary—Renaissance garden architects created something unique which we refer to generically as "the Italian garden." Terraces, steps, and water channels on the steep Tuscan hillsides formed long vistas and shady axial compositions embracing views over the city or the nearby countryside. Staircases acted as links, instead of being freestanding or isolated as they were in the ancient world. Unity of composition was sought and the harmony of parts carefully measured. Especially new was the unity of house and garden. In literature, turning to Greece and Rome, the poet-scholar Boccaccio had set the tone, reading the Greek and Latin authors far into the night, but in his time the garden was still a roofless room and scarcely bigger than one. It contained a fountain, turf benches, and an arbor, all typical of the medieval pleasance, with sometimes a bowling green and orchard as accompaniments. Boccaccio's description of the Villa Palmieri (formerly Schifanoia) in the introduction to the third day of the *Decameron* (1348) is somewhat more fanciful. The walks and alleys were long and spacious, environed with spreading vines. In the middle was a square plot like a meadow, grown high with grass and flowers. There were fruit and cedar trees around and a fountain in the middle. Although the garden still exists, all traces of the original layout have disappeared; the oldest part is now an oval lemon garden dating from the late seventeenth century.

Backing the new architecture and the new garden art was a rising business culture. This patronage was something the medieval world had not encouraged, although it is not wise to suggest that the Renaissance made a sudden break-through, since commerce had been increasing in the thirteenth and fourteenth centuries. The support lent by business enabled the individual to discover himself; henceforth the human body and the human mind were celebrated in a way that had not been possible until the collapse of feudalism, a system which omitted the merchants and townsmen and their money economy from its philosophy. Academies founded by merchant- and banker-princes flourished. The Fete of the Intellect was held in the palace of Lorenzo the Magnificent, whose poetry and interest in gardening are both well known. Toward the end of the fifteenth

A LESS WELL KNOWN ITALIAN VILLA. The Villa Cicogna ("stork") lies between the city of Varese and Lake Lugano. It belongs to Count Carlo Cicogna Mazzoni, whose family has owned it for four hundred years. The gardens date from the period after 1600. In addition to such "Italian

garden" features as a water staircase, grotto, and enclosed gallery masked by a retaining wall, there is near the top of the hill an early nineteenth-century "bosco Inglese" with stone seats in clearings, affording distant views over the Lombard countryside.

century the famous Orti Orcellari at Florence were laid out by Bernardo Rucellai, the kinsman of Lorenzo. Here it was that the celebrated Platonic Academy held its meetings and Niccolò Machiavelli read his discourses. By the second half of the sixteenth century, when the importation of plants from Constantinople had begun what later eventuated in a constant succession of floral novelties from all over the world, lovers of gardening had tulips, anemones, and other flowers to hybridize and send to friends all over Europe. The garden of simples was transformed into a Persian carpet and the freemasonry of horticulture brought about a communication between classes and countrymen that had never before existed.[4]

The private garden and the private park became recognized as elements in the designer's *vade mecum*, drawing from a classical past and proliferating all over Europe, as kings and princes, nobility and gentry, merchants and burghers vied with one another in creating beautiful surroundings out-of-doors. We see the young Louis XIV of France resolving during a garden fete at Vaux le Vicomte to surpass this triumph of his minister Fouquet by creating an even vaster composition, based on the legend of Apollo, in the unprepossessing swamps and woods of Versailles. This prodigious enterprise, enormous in size compared with any garden or park then to be seen in Italy, was dedicated entirely to pleasure. "All who were 'reasonably dressed' were admitted to the park, and countrymen's carts jostled those of noblemen."[5] There was little privacy at court, but springing up in Paris were intimate, smaller gardens in the classical manner, walled, and attached to the new *hôtels* that the nobility were building for themselves.

Prototypes of the axial vista, on either side of which Versailles and Vaux le Vicomte display their garden treasures, could of course be found in Italy at an earlier date, although they were quite rudimentary compared with the classical French examples. The Quaracchi villa near Florence and another mid-fifteenth century Tuscan garden, that of the Cafagglio, laid out by the flower-loving Lorenzo, both had elementary axes directed toward the river. One can likewise discern in the streets leading from the Piazza del Popolo of Sixtus V a possible influence on the plan of the town of Versailles.

With Vaux le Vicomte we come upon a new type of artist, the professional designer of gardens, in the person of André Lenôtre (1613–1700), himself the son

One of the architect Le Blond's many designs for a *parterre de broderie*. The artist was a pupil of Lenôtre. ➤

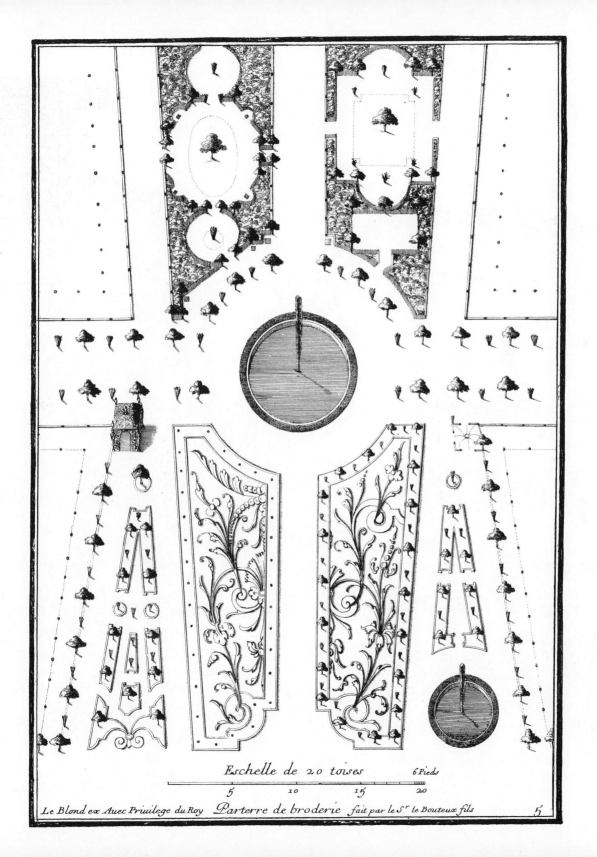

Eschelle de 20 toises   6 Pieds

5   10   15   20

Le Blond ex Auec Priuilege du Roy   Parterre de broderie faí par le Sʳ le Bouteux fils   5

THE TAMING OF WILD NATURE. AN ANTECEDENT OF THE LANDSCAPE GARDEN. At the end of the fifteenth century a monk of Milan, one Bernadino Caimi, built a New Jerusalem on a small mountain near Varallo in northern Italy. A road winds up the hill, passing forty-five chapels, all different and each embodying some part of the gospel story. These little buildings are richly decorated and filled inside with life-sized figures (seen through

grilles) which seem startlingly real because many of them were made by prominent artists of the day. This New Jerusalem was not the last miniature pantheon to be built on a man-molded landscape: Stourhead in England and other estates of amateur landscape gardeners in the eighteenth century were dotted with small temples, "all mossy, mythological marble" and dedicated to the muses or the ancient virtues.

of a famous gardener to the court. After Lenôtre, a "familiar" as well as an employee of Louis XIV, the profession became accepted, thanks largely to the worldwide fame of Lenôtre's work at Versailles. After that time we hear of garden designers by name, making it possible to give more positive attributions in this often ephemeral form of art.

Some of Lenôtre's near contemporaries in England have only recently been rescued from relative obscurity by art historians, forgotten in the cult of the "informal" English landscape school. (That school, incidentally, was responsible for the destruction of the chief examples of the classical style. Aerial photography has helped in tracing the plans of these old gardens on the ground.[6]) Hussey calls Charles Bridgeman (date of birth and parentage unknown) the counterpart of Lenôtre in England. He was regarded not as a tradesman to be paid from state accounts, but as being on a par with architects. Stowe in Buckinghamshire retains the impress of his early plan, but of the dozens of estates with which he is known to have been connected "the majority are obliterated or almost unrecognisably altered."[7]

No sooner had the art of garden design been recognized than it went through a sea change, with a fresh wind from the Pacific blowing through the courts of Europe. This was the news of the Chinese way of looking at gardens, which had a certain affinity with their methods of landscape painting. The French took this novelty in their stride, but the English began to develop the irregular garden, which in turn became the landscape garden, spreading its message not only to the rest of Europe but all over the world as well.

The Case for Sharawadji

The word first appears in Sir William Temple's essay, "On the Gardens of Epicurus," published in 1685. The significant passage follows:

> The Chineses scorn this way of planting, and say that a boy that can count an hundred may plant walks of trees in straight lines, and over against one another, and to what length and extent he pleases. But their greatest reach of imagination is employed in contriving figures, where the beauty shall be

great, and strike the eye, but without any order or disposition of parts that shall be commonly or easily observed; and though we have hardly any notion of this sort of beauty, yet they have a particular word to express it, and where they find it hit their eye at first sight, they say the *sharawadji* is fine or admirable, or any such expression of esteem. And whoever observes the work upon the best India gowns, or the painting upon their best screens or porcelains, will find their beauty is all of this kind (that is) without order. But I should hardly advise any of these attempts in the figure of gardens among us; they are adventures of too hard achievement for any common hands; and though there may be more honour if they succeed well, yet there is more dishonour if they fail, and it is twenty to one they will; whereas in regular figures it is hard to make any great and remarkable faults.[8]

Temple had been a diplomat at The Hague, where he had had an opportunity to see and learn of Chinese art, the Dutch having recently sent an embassy to Peking, a member of which, John Nieuhoff, had written an account of the expedition. Translated into French and English, it contained a description of the Chinese landscape garden of the Imperial Palace. But the word *Sharawadji* was new, and many people deemed it simply an invention of Temple's.

Y. Z. Chang,[9] writing some years ago, traced the term to *sa-ro-(k)wai-chi* ("graceful disorder"). There is a Japanese word also, *sorowaji* ("not being regular"), which perhaps derives from it. Chang maintains that it is several words run together, and cites as an example the epithet "Damn you, fool," which is known in China, for those who do not speak English, as *Dam-you-foolo*. This is sometimes changed into one word, *damiofulu*. *Sharawadji* means "the quality of being impressive or surprising through careless or unorderly grace." Chang concludes that one cannot blame the *Oxford English Dictionary* for inability to deal with it; only to blame was the deplorable state of sinology in Europe, which meant that nobody at the time was qualified to give help.

Sharawadji is therefore an exotic term, befitting the English notion of a fabulous land of Cathay, which bore little relation to the mundane China finally revealed by nineteenth-century travellers like Robert Fortune. As for Japan, the Portuguese had been there as early as 1542, profiting from a Sino-Japanese war, but in 1638 they were expelled or accepted martyrdom when the Japanese discovered the exclusive nature of Christianity, and only the Dutch were allowed to remain on an island off Nagasaki. In the eighteenth century Japan was thought of as a dim part of the Chinese empire. What Temple saw or heard remains conjectural, apart from the porcelain and textiles he mentions in the above-quoted passage. It is possible that he had seen Chinese paintings, since John Evelyn, writing in 1664, claims that a Jesuit, one Thompson, had shown *him* "prints of landscapes."[10]

We are indebted to Basil Gray of the British Museum, who in 1960 offered proof that visual as well as verbal evidence of Chinese gardens was available to Burlington's circle (which in this context means William Kent, the father of English landscape gardening, who lived in that superb patron's household).[11] Gray established the fact that a copy of Father Ripa's engraved garden views, now in the Museum, had come originally from the Chiswick House Library.[12] Gray thinks that the novelty of Kent's viewpoint may have attracted him to these views of Jehol, marking a *point d'appui* in the development of English taste. This conjecture was followed by Wittkower in 1969,[13] and it is observable that there is a somewhat irregular section of Kent's design for the Chiswick House grounds, but although presumably available to Kent, the Ripa engravings remained in the Burlington circle, whereas Temple's verbal account was quoted throughout the eighteenth century.

Temple may have put the "difficult new idea" into practice at his Moor Park in Surrey (not to be confused with the more famous Moor Park in Hertfordshire, after which it was named). The late Christopher Hussey unearthed for his last book a perspective view of Temple's garden, done about 1690, Hussey thought, which shows a part outside the main grounds with curvilinear walks most unusual for the time. Otherwise, the gardens are quite formally Dutch, a manner of planting Temple had admired at The Hague.

By 1712, Temple, now dead, had an important advocate. Addison's *Spectator* essay of June 25 in that year is a paraphrase without acknowledgement of the Temple passage. Without mentioning *Sharawadji*, Addison wrote: "They have a word for it, it seems, in their language, by which they express the particular beauty of a plantation," adding, "Writers who have given us an account of China tell us that the inhabitants of that country laugh at the plantations of Europeans."

Irregularity was becoming *avant garde*; soon Pope was planting his garden at Twickenham, of which nothing remains but the bare bones of his grotto and the plan drawn up in 1745 after his death by his gardener Serle.

Addison's attack on the mathematical precision of English garden design has been called the most significant fact of eighteenth-century esthetics, if only because he was a powerful conservative authority whose opinions were followed by a great many people. "Our English gardens are not so entertaining to the Fancy as those in France and Italy," he wrote, "where we see a large Extent of Ground covered over with an agreeable mixture of Garden and Forest, which represent everywhere an artificial Rudeness, much more charming than that Neatness and Elegancy which we meet with in those of our own Country." This may seem odd, considering the formality of earlier European gardens, but the current revival of garden scholarship shows that what had happened to the French and especially the Italian garden was the freer Baroque planting of the seventeenth century, which had created the great park gardens of Rome, a city in which natural scenery had become a new inspiration.[14] What more logical than that Kent, who had been there, and the amateur gardening milords who had already borrowed so much from Italy, should borrow once more when it came to planting their estates?

And in 1728 appeared Robert Castell's *The Villas of the Ancients*, which took the landscape garden back to the ancient Romans. The younger Pliny, this author declared, had gardens in which "hills, rocks, cascades, rivulets, woods and buildings . . . were possibly thrown into such a disorder as to have pleased the eye from several views, like so many beautiful landskips." Certainly at least one of Pliny's villas had an extremely beautiful site on Lake Como, later evoked by Shelley in terms of an English landscape garden.[15]

By the mid-eighteenth century, when chinoiserie is at its height, we have three important justifications for the new gardening: *Sharawadji*, which deified irregularity and became a casual label for naturalistic esthetics; painting in the neoclassic manner and other gardening traditions absorbed in Italy; and nature itself as described by Milton and later poets like Thompson, who thought it better not simply to copy nature (whatever that meant) but to improve on it with cunning artifice—to make it look more like itself, so to speak.

Still, the idea that China was the original inspiration is very sympathetic, even though it is now thoroughly out of fashion. That was not the case in the mid-eighteenth century: "Our farms and seats begin / To match the boasted villas of Pekin," wrote James Cawthorn in 1756, at the height of the oriental craze.[16] The chinoiserie of the 1750s was no sudden growth. Chinese rooms, painted panels, tapestries, and wallpaper were all to be found in late seventeenth-century England. Imported oriental wallpapers showed zigzag fences, mountainous prospects, flimsy wooden buildings, and mustachioed rural inhabitants. These wallpapers were also imported into North America by merchants like Thomas Hancock in 1738. Fretted work had appeared on garden fences in America as early as 1702.[17] One rich nabob and East India Company official, Elihu Yale, had brought back to England in 1699, the year of Temple's death, a collection of Mogul miniatures; in 1700, at the Soho factories, Chinese tapestries were woven for him. His own set is in the Yale University Art Gallery. The English weavers' imagination is well shown there, but at the same time so much genuine eastern fabric was introduced between 1690 and 1700 that for a while the London weavers were out of work.

India became more familiar to Europeans after the advent of the East India Company. India, China, and Japan formed one vast philosophical whole, representing for many a civilization different from, but not necessarily inferior to, that of the West. Hence the physiocrats, Voltaire's Chinese plays, and the theories of Leibnitz, none of which was destined to last very long.

Enter the French. Having supplied—with the Dutch, of course—much of the *raison d'etre* for *Sharawadji* in the seventeenth century (it was largely the French Jesuit missionaries who were responsible for the legend of Cathay), they took up the new English style of gardening in mid-century, especially after the Trianon de Porcelaine appeared in 1670–71. Frenchmen couldn't believe that so delightful a conceit could have been invented by sports-loving, pig-sticking English squires. As Horace Walpole commented in 1771, "The French have of late years adopted our style in gardens, but, choosing to be fundamentally obliged to more remote rivals, they deny us half the merit or rather the originality of the invention, by ascribing the discovery to the Chinese, and calling our taste in gardening *le gout anglo-chinois*." Walpole's remarks may have been inspired by French topo-

Elihu Yale, an English nabob known as the founder of Yale College, commissioned the two rare chinoiserie tapestries by John Vanderbank from the Soho works which are now in the Yale University Art Gallery. This one is called *The Promenade*.

Governor William Paca's garden at Annapolis, which was recently restored. The Chinese bridge, designed by Orin Bullock after the evidence of a Charles Willson Peale portrait of Paca in his garden, is seen in the lower part of the photograph.

graphical historians like Le Rouge, who in 1776 began to publish his quartos on European gardens, noting in the introduction, "Everyone knows that the English garden is only an imitation of those of China." "It is to these Chinese gardens that the English owe their reputation," wrote the Prince de Ligne in 1781. Asseverations like these had caused the poet Gray, friend of Mason and Walpole, to exclaim twenty years earlier, "It is not forty years since the art was born among us; and it is sure there was nothing in Europe like it, and as sure that we had no information on this head from China"—a belief hotly contested by sinologues to this day.

With several exceptions, like the Marquis de Girardin's Ermenonville (an entire "walking-around" garden, as an Oriental would call it, containing the erstwhile tomb of Rousseau), the French tended to keep the anglo-chinois garden as a separate entity, attached to the Lenôtre-style parterre gardens, which, unlike the followers of Lancelot Brown, they tended to keep and not sweep away in the tide of parkomania. But the Chinese taste penetrated even the grounds of Versailles, and in the 1770s Horace Walpole, who by then was the father of the Gothic novel and the Gothic taste in architecture, paid France a visit to confirm his fears. He saw that the French had been confused, as he thought, by the translation of Sir William Chambers's *Dissertation on Oriental Gardening*, which had had some success on the Continent. "The French totally misunderstand the basic principles of the new English style," Walpole observed. Elsewhere he wrote, "I can find nothing in the Chinese emperor's pleasure ground which gives me any idea of attention being paid to nature."

It is not likely that Chambers, who had been in China and was the architect of the neoclassic and beautiful Somerset House, as well as the Chinese pagoda at Kew, expected his exaggerated scenes of dragons in caves and Chinese bandits hiding therein to be copied in English gardens. Unlike the poet William Mason, who taught the lessons of horticulture through the romance of Alcander and Nerine in an English landscape garden, he probably hoped to confound the British complacent acceptance of shaved lawns and Brownian tree clumps.[18] And we must not forget the extravagances of his detractors, including Walpole, who allowed that the sham Gothic castle at Hagley "had the true rust of the barons' wars."[19] It was only a scant three years before, in 1750, that Walpole had written to Horace Mann, "I am almost as fond of the Sharrawaggi, or Chinese want of symmetry, in buildings, as in grounds or gardens." He was still searching for a term to describe the beauties of irregularity, but in the same year confided to friends that he intended "to build a little Gothic castle at Strawberry Hill." Walpole found it easier to reconcile, or perhaps to reinforce, his writings on British history and British worthies with sham Gothic rather than sham Orient, and it is no real surprise that he turned so violently against the Chinese taste in gardens. By 1762 he is writing to George Montague, "I did not doubt that you would approve Mr. Bateman's estate, since it has changed its religion. I converted it from Chinese to Gothic." Twenty years later he is still pleased with the result. He reminisces, "I am proud of having converted Dicky Bateman from a Chinese to a Goth. Though he was the founder of the Sharawadji taste in England I preached so effectually that his every pagoda took the veil."

Chambers had an unexpected supporter in his friend Oliver Goldsmith. The poet thought that Chinese gardening in "a very small extent of ground is enough for an elegant taste." He wrote to Chambers in 1773: "Most of the companies that I now go into divide themselves into two parties, the Chamberists and ye Brownists, but depend upon it you'll in the end have Victory, because you have Truth and Nature on your side. Mr. Burke was advising me about four days ago to draw my pen in a poem in defense of your system, and sincerely, I am very much warmed in the Cause."[20] But Goldsmith died the next year, having witnessed more than one deserted village. "Capability Brown" was anathema: when Goldsmith had visited Chatsworth he saw that Brown had removed half the village of Edensor; he had done the same thing at Audley End; and at Warwick Castle he had demolished a village so that he could landscape both sides of the river Avon. There were many more crimes, including the removal of the village of West Sheen when Brown reshaped Richmond Park. Goldsmith preferred to cite Chambers's more sympathetic work at Kew, where the Kew villagers (who had not been removed) came to praise the clemency of Augusta's gardening ("Ode on the Death of Princess Augusta," 1772).

Of course, Chambers did not have victory in the affair, in spite of his popularity at court and his Swedish Order of the Polar Star. Who could stand up against Horace Walpole in the cultural circles of the eighteenth century? Besides, one can easily see that Gothic gloom and tales of terror not only suited the English

ECCENTRIC TASTE IN GARDENING. On the hillside beyond the sixteenth-century garden of the luxurious Villa d'Este on Lake Como, long since a hotel but justly famed for its magnificent water staircase and classical air, rises a series of miniature fortresses and battlements all connected by walks, steps, and crenellated walls. These latter are the creation of the wife of a Napoleonic general, Count Domenico Pino, who knew that her husband's first love was the army and wished to keep him at home; indeed, it is recorded that he was delighted with the mock towers and recruited a corps of small boys to engage in military maneuvers on this wild terrain.

CHINOISERIE NEARS ITS END. A sketch of the garden at Alton Towers in Shropshire, showing the pagoda fountain.

temperament better than brightly painted wooden buildings with tinkly bells under the eaves, crooked bridges, and Nanking pagodas, but that Gothic fell in with the romantic mood which would sweep Europe in the early years of the next century. Only a few Chinese monuments appeared in England in the Romantic period—the charming pagoda fountain at Alton Towers and, of course, the Brighton Pavilion, completed in 1821, which had a Hindu exterior and a chinoiserie interior, and in which George IV was wont to entertain his guests in a loud baritone, assisted by an orchestra of seventy musicians.

Walpole is the last important eighteenth-century figure to use the term *Sharawadji*. I have found it again in Mrs. Loudon's 1860 edition of her husband's *Encyclopaedia of Gardening*, which quotes Sir William Temple and describes the then-novel accounts of Robert Fortune's Chinese explorations. What the nineteenth century imported from the East was not an esthetic notion but hundreds of plants new to Europe—forsythias, Chinese rhododendrons, wisterias, tree peonies—an importation which is now being tentatively revived in the form of seed exchange. Apart from that, we are today more interested in China's politics and social programs than in the natural theology of Confucianism, which had such an extraordinary vogue among the eighteenth-century pundits of Europe. Landscape worship was something entirely new in the eighteenth century, and the English translated it in terms of their beloved fields and streams. They could not understand Chinese landscape gardening because they had not seen it. The Chinese were indeed landscape gardeners, but in the sense that their intent was to evoke feelings for the natural landscape and to attune the mind to nature's rhythmical round, whereas the aim of the English landscape garden after Kent was to make the garden part of the landscape, merging it into the surrounding scenery as much as possible. The Chinese end product was to give expression to a poetical or religious dream, an approach far from the mind of the noblemen who employed Kent, Brown, and Humphry Repton. Had they seen a contemporary garden in China, they would have been repelled by what they would have considered to be its garish, muddled, and contorted look, so different from the smooth turf and wide-open sweep of the English hunting park. They had at first only a funny-sounding word to guide them, and it is astonishing that it haunted them for so long.

Critics and Admirers

The inspiration of sentiment and irregularity lingered in France, at Bagatelle, and in a dozen places shown in the plans of Le Rouge. Bagatelle is much altered, as are most of the late eighteenth-century gardens of poetical inspiration, if indeed they have not completely disappeared. The best-known and the best-preserved, although lacking some of its former embellishments, is Ermenonville, where Rousseau spent the last months of his life as a guest of his patron, the Marquis de Girardin, studying botany. The great nature lover did not, however, advise the marquis to leave nature alone. He pointed out in *La Nouvelle Héloïse* that for Europeans who loved nature but could not travel to distant mountain tops or deserts "where she spreads her most ravishing charms . . . nothing remains but to

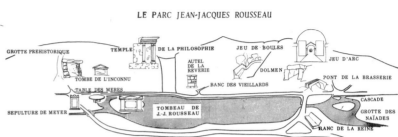

LE PARC JEAN-JACQUES ROUSSEAU

Rousseau spent the last months of his life botanizing at Ermenonville, the estate of the Marquis de Girardin. This plan shows what is left of the objects to be seen. The marquis had the advice of the English poet Shenstone in laying out the grounds.

Rousseau's tomb on the Ile des Peupliers.

do violence to Nature and to force her to take up her abode with (those who love her); and *this cannot be done without a certain illusion*" (italics mine).

It is still possible to evoke the spirit of Ermenonville *mutatis mutandis* when walking around the park. The planting, which benefits from the lush, marshy site watered by the river Launette,[21] is now romantically overgrown. Giant *platanus* sweep their branches down to the surface of the artificial lake, filtering the sunlight through their pale leaves. In the woods all is somber around the Philosophers' Temple (one of its columns is dedicated to William Penn and one to Benjamin Franklin) and the monument A la Reverie for young and old loves. The Promenade d'Ermenonville is almost as delightful as ever; one misses the Tour de Gabrielle on the north side of the chateau (dedicated to none other than Gabrielle d'Estrées) more for its former eye-catching qualities than for its rather farfetched associative message. The grounds are well maintained by the present owners, the Touring Club of France, and the chateau is now a hotel which the public can enter for the price of a meal.

The neoclassic commemorative garden fades and reappears again in a more romantic form in the work of J. J. Ramée, Thomas Jefferson, and John Nash.[22] But the style "which had come to be associated with English and Chinese thought"[23] had lasted for a hundred years, since the magic of *Sharawadji* had first attracted the West. It was not "natural," and the proponents of the new Brownian school, followed by the devotees of the picturesque, scorned the artificial. The peak had been reached, rather than a preliminary to what was to come. Henceforth, gardens were to avoid the excesses of "bad taste."

Seen through other than English eyes, the landscape garden is divested of its aura of sanctity, either through overpraise or ridicule. Two European noblemen, both notable designers of gardens themselves, were firsthand observers of the English park at the turn of the nineteenth century and after. The Prince de Ligne is an eighteenth-century figure who lived long enough to see the Congress of Vienna; Prince Pückler-Muskau also was there, but lived on until 1871. The two men had but one thing in common besides a love of gardens: they were both great amorists. Pückler-Muskau was a dedicated Brownian. His business in England in the year 1826 was to find an heiress wife, but the heiresses were wont to decline his proposals when they discovered that he had only divorced his wife Lucie in order to recoup his fortunes abroad; indeed he hated to be parted from her for long. He travelled extensively in the British Isles, declared himself to be a victim of "parkomanie," and exclaimed when he saw Blenheim, "One cannot help admiring the grandeur of Brown's genius and conceptions, as one wanders through these grounds: he is the Shakespeare of gardening."[24] One may perhaps be permitted to think that the original plan for Blenheim by Henry Wise, with its bastion garden walls and monumental avenue, would have been more sympathetic to Vanbrugh's majestic palace for the Iron Duke.[25]

Brown would not have liked the carpet bedding (a delightful conceit in hothouse flowers) that the prince introduced near the house at Muskau. Defeated after many tries in his fortune-hunting endeavors in England, he was eventually forced to sell his huge Silesian estates, in which he had created a great river park, and retire to a smaller one at Branitz. Here, after accruing numerous honors in later life, he was buried beneath a giant pyramid standing in a lake. He had planned this himself, inspired by the Koran: "Graves are the mountain-tops of a distant, lovely land," an appropriate inscription for one who admired beauty in all surrounding him.

While the English must have thought of Pückler-Muskau as something of a Mephistopheles, so devastating were his comments on their class system, the Prince de Ligne was a different case. His insouciance and good manners charmed all who met him, and he reveled in his lifelong pursuit of the love of beautiful and famous women. He lost his garden at Beloeil, fleeing the revolution (it is now being tastefully restored by his descendant and is well worth a visit). Here is a man who built himself a Temple of Truth and opposite it a Temple of Illusion, the latter being perhaps more to his taste, since it is not easy to distinguish between fact and fancy in his *Coup d'Oeil sur Beloeil*. There were bosquets dedicated to his friends, but de Ligne did not intend that nature should swallow its lovers in informal thickets of bushes and trees. "I should be sorry to get rid of straight lines," he advised, "for they are the means of achieving great things." There were springs in his park which provided enough water for a cascade and a great canal; he mentions a Chinese temple (to be used as a pigeon house), a mausoleum of

Adonis, and a Garden of the Philosophers. He liked the place to be full of people. On the morning after his son's marriage, the bridal couple woke up to find a huge fete in progress outside their windows—shepherds and shepherdesses from the estate were enjoying the sideshows, and the Ligne infantry (the prince was a famous commander of soldiery), dressed in their rose-colored uniforms, were singing the praises of the bride.[26]

De Ligne was a favorite at the court of Versailles, where he said life was like a country house party. He befriended Du Barry, who had been his mistress, when she was deserted by the court after the death of Louis XV. He saw the whole pageant of court life fade and vanish utterly, but not before he had indeed seen everything. "I have seen three weeks of magic fetes at Chantilly," he recalled in his memoirs, mentioning that he admired the gardens there more than those of Versailles. "I have seen the enchanted voyages of Isle-Adam; I have seen the delights of the Petit-Trianon, the walks on the Terrace, the music in the Orangery, the splendor of Fontainebleau, the hunts of St. Hubert and of Choisy."[27] He saw also the great gardens of Catherine the Great in Russia and the glories of Potsdam and Sans Souci. On his own garden he spent perhaps 500,000 florins, not excessive he thought, and he entertained as generously as his reduced means allowed in Vienna, where, when he died in 1815, the whole Congress attended his funeral.

The author of *Beloeil*, who in his own park preferred to mingle the heroic with the seductive, had much to say about the new English landscape garden. He was curious about the lawn-based parks of "Capability Brown," observing that the islanders had made splendid use of their climate to grow grass ("their verdure they owe to their fogs"). However, he believed, that same climate prevented the realization of the true ambiance of such gardens, which derived from the *Eclogues*. In vain did the visiting prince listen for the sound of the flute among the clumpish groves, and he found the shepherds not so gentle as their sheep. The true sentiments of Horace and Virgil, he thought, could only be echoed in warmer countries. "The shade, the well-spaced clumps of trees, their mass, the shafts of light between them, and the joy of overcoming difficulties would recompense me in the southern provinces of France for the verdure of England." And he condemned the English "atrabilious milords" for not doing enough in creating their new parks, which he found to be "merely deserts, wild places and pure savagery." Those little pools that were passed off as rivers he found childish in the extreme.

"The means Brown used were as sparse as the patterns he made with them were simple. Contours of green turf, mirrors of still water, a few species of tree used singly or in clumps or in loosely-contrived belts—and that was all," writes a recent historian[28] who is an admirer of what Christopher Hussey has called the "pure landscape." He goes on to say that the English park garden was attempted all over Europe, but did not export well. As the prince had observed, a green velvety lawn and lush tree growth is a prerequisite, and the combination is not attainable everywhere. I have seen very few "Englisher" gardens which are attractive enough to stand as compositions in their own right: among these are the Kaiser park at Bad Ischl and the Empress Eugenie's English park above the town at Saint Cloud. Neither of these goes as far as Brown did to sacrifice everything to the lawn—at Claremeont he hid the servants' entrance in a tunnel underground to preserve an unbroken green sweep around the house.

> The terrace sinks spontaneous; on the green,
> Broidered with crisp knots, the tonsile yews
> Wither and fall; the fountain dares no more
> To fling its wasted crystals through the sky,
> But pours salubrious o'er the parched lawn
> Rills of fertility. —Oh! blest of Arts
> That works this happy change!

[William Mason, *The English Garden*, 1771–81]

But with nothing left except the lawn and its undulations the garden had been denuded of its chief attractions.

> Wrapt all o'er in everlasting green
> Makes one dull vapid smooth and tranquil scene.

[Richard Payne Knight, *The Landscape*, 1794]

The heart of the matter was the denial of the classical spirit, which garden design had reembraced quite early in the Renaissance. The Gothic revival had begun and was to remain especially fashionable in gardens, with Strawberry Hill as a model. The Prince de Ligne had no love for Horace Walpole's sham gothic: "the Gothick [buildings] of Mr. Walpole, I am tempted to believe were inspired by the delirium of a nightmare. I liked his castle of Otranto: but this one on the Thames is just as silly, and not so amusing."[29] The garden of sentiment had at least contained elements of classic derivation, even though veering toward the "Chinese." As it was, the formal garden near the house was revived by Humphry Repton, and in 1805 Richard Payne Knight's "Enquiry" recommended "the hanging terraces of Italian gardens" as being the perfect base for the house to stand on. "Another revolution in taste," Knight surmised, "will make them new again."

Well before the mid-nineteenth century the Italian garden was back in England, this time floriferous with the new plant discoveries from abroad. But far too many of the old formal gardens had been swept away by the Improvers. As late as the 1830s whole stretches of territory were still being transformed into "natural" parks, not only in England but elsewhere. In faraway Australia, one Thomas Shepherd introduced Reptonain theories in a series of lectures on landscape gardening, the first of which was given at the Mechanics' School of Arts in Sydney in 1835. Shepherd owned a nursery, but professed a knowledge of design through earlier experience in laying out grounds in England. Although full of praise for Repton, he nevertheless was not averse to showing up Repton's lack of technical skill. While laying out an estate in Kent, Shepherd recalled, he found that Repton was doing the same thing in an adjoining property. The dissatisfied proprietor called in Shepherd (according to Shepherd himself), who found that "the place was as rough as a ploughed field—a good design entirely ruined." Repton, brought to see the younger man's grading and leveling, exclaimed, "I never saw work completed in this style in all my life; I cannot perform work like this." Shepherd advised him to employ a competent superintendent accustomed to leveling land, whereupon Repton thanked him for his advice, saying that "if he could execute work like mine, he might keep his carriage and live independent" (although Repton's charges were ten guineas a day and traveling expenses, Shepherd tells us, "he died poor. . . . He never kept company but with men of rank").

A bookplate found in one of Humphry Repton's unique Red Books (bound in red morocco), now in the rare book collection of Yale University. A manuscript volume written in a formal script, it is addressed to Lord Whitworth and entitled "Hints, Plans and Sketches for the Improvement of Stonelands in Sussex."

Shepherd advised the crown squatters and new landed proprietors to acquire about seven thousand acres, keeping one thousand for the mansion and park. His advice against indiscriminate cutting of trees is well put; otherwise his suggestions follow Repton without deviation, down to the provision of such embellishments near the house as aviaries and flower gardens for the ladies. While Shepherd dispenses sensible advice about keeping much of the natural cover, in all his seven lectures there is no reference to a specific native Eucalypt or even a Moreton Bay

Fig, specimens of which are such a distinctive feature of the Sydney landscape today; the whole concept is a transplant from British soil, even to its flattering references to scions of nobility, whom Shepherd hoped to attract to New South Wales. He is admiring of the Honorable Alexander M'Leay's estate at Elizabeth Bay (M'Leay was an important public servant and amateur botanist) but was not above suggesting that it could be improved by the addition of an ornamental summer house, a pinery, an aviary, and a conservatory.[30]

So spread the English landscape garden around the world as an exportable commodity. Enthusiastic gardeners though they are, Australians have only recently begun to appreciate what the "bush" provides in the way of horticultural rewards.

The Picturesque Syndrome

Garden design as "a work of art using the materials of nature," as Repton described his craft, is important as a vehicle for experiments in the picturesque, easily transferrable to architecture, and not quite so easily to town planning, where straight lines on the whole are easier to manipulate. No matter that Wordsworth decried the landscape gardeners—among the undulations of spongy turf they gave shape to picturesque and romantic ideas which suited the changing times. Some people have seen in this the seeds of decay, crediting the landscape garden with contributing to the decline of architecture and the exaltation of a nature cult, in which a diffuseness of form and feeling replaces older, stronger beliefs.[31] Even Goethe, who praised Pückler-Muskau to the skies, and who loved to stroll in the Englisher Garten of the Duke of Anhalt in Dessau, saying that it suggested to him the Elysian Fields, was forced to admit that "there is no central point any longer given at which we may look."

With Repton, who was followed by Barry, Paxton, and Nesfield in England, and Downing, Olmsted, and Vaux in the United States, the nineteenth century reintroduced the flowers that Brown had banished. Perhaps the Empress Josephine, in compensation for a lost throne, had played her part by cultivating and making popular the rose at Malmaison, but above all it was the "botanical travellers," as Joseph Banks called them, who provided Western countries with a newfound flora, so that J. C. Loudon, in 1825, could record that Europe grew thirteen thousand species and varieties, nearly a quarter of the estimated flora of the whole world.[32] One hundred and fifty years later the search for new varieties goes on, and an amateur interest in horticulture flourishes.

By the 1840s writers on gardening, including the prolific Mr. and Mrs. Loudon, were addressing themselves to women. In the beginning of that decade Mrs. Loudon produced her *Instructions in Gardening for Ladies*, which "encouraged delicate Victorian ladies to abandon their lace shawls for hessian aprons, their needles for spades, and their plush sofas for 'the reviving smell of fresh earth.' "[33] While it is too much to say that gardening has been in the hands of women ever since, this period marks the end of their being only seen in gardens, which once served merely as a setting for courtship or domestic bliss. "If the American farmer has no taste for flowers," observed William Cobett in 1829, "his wife and daughters may." It was women who brought along treasured plants on the American move westward across the continent, accounting, among other survivals, for the now-ancient specimens of remontant tea roses to be found in California and Oregon.

With Loudon, the emphasis is put on flower beds and bedding plants, causing acrimonious battles to begin between different kinds of flower lovers, as we shall see in a moment. It was all very well for Mrs. Loudon to say (in a new edition of her late husband's *Suburban Gardener*) that "any lady who can design a pattern, and embroider a gown, might . . . in a few hours, be taught to design flower gardens with as much skill and taste as a landscape gardener," but Mrs. Loudon's flower garden, which was slightly more geometrical than Pückler-Muskau's cornucopias, was to fall into disfavor among "women of taste." It had a good run for its money, as anyone who has enjoyed the intricacies of the Loudon-inspired carpet or subtropical bedding in public parks can testify. The primary colors—red (geraniums), yellow (calceolarias), and blue (lobelias)—were admired by mid-Victorians; richness was what they desired and richness was certainly achieved in well-displayed ribbons of summer bedding, but such effects came to be despised as the years wore on and new fashions in horticulture appeared.

In overall design the nineteenth-century garden takes several forms, albeit the

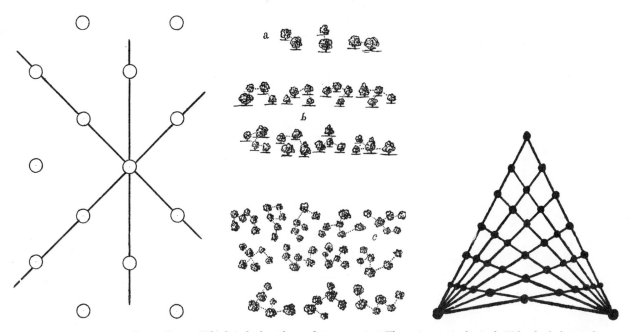

MORE THAN ONE WAY TO PLANT TREES. Which is the best form of tree grouping? The quincunx is classical. "What looks better than a quincunx layout which is in line every way you look?" asks Sir Thomas Browne. "It is an aspect of the planets." Coleridge thought it was a network like that seen in optic nerves. Very different were the opinions held by landscape gardener Andrew Jackson Downing. The smallest grouping, he observed, was of two trees, but they could be seen in three different positions by the spectator; with six trees there were twelve possible positions. Downing changed the taste of villadom in the United States in the first half of the nineteenth century and led the vanguard of picturesque fashion. But even he was without the ingenuity of today's mathematician who could puzzle his readers by asking them to arrange 38 trees in 12 rows with 7 trees in a row.

picturesque syndrome is apt to influence all of them (it being first advocated in print in the mid-eighteenth century by William Gilpin, who, as we have seen, journeyed to find picturesque beauty in British natural landscapes). A classical garden in Victorian times is apt to contain picturesque incidents, and most gardens and parks give themselves entirely to picturesque forms. Some mid-century parks grudgingly include a few classical elements—the Mall in Central Park, for instance—and it is to features like this and like the park's well-known fountain and staircase that the mind returns when focusing on the park's design.

The landscape garden (pure) was not forgotten as the nineteenth century progressed (in fact, Pückler-Muskau found "parkomanie" extending well beyond the mid-century mark), but its influence became ludicrous when employed on tiny

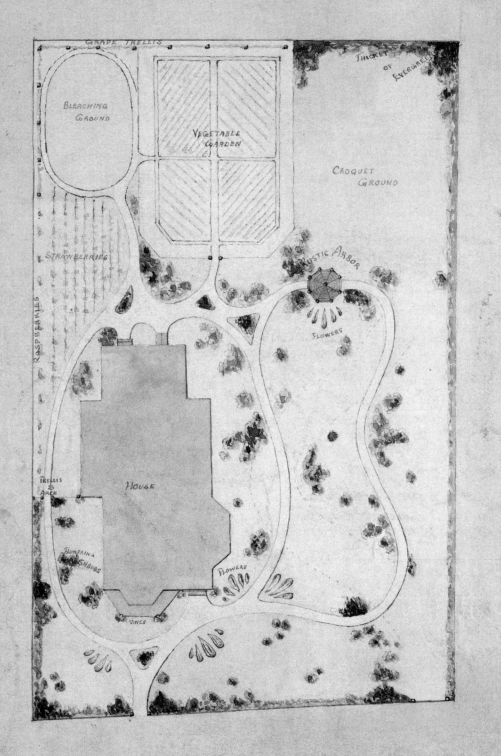

A plan of a New Haven town garden, designed after the manner of Andrew Jackson Downing. It was found in the attic of a house built before 1853.

plots of land which made up the suburban mosaic. Realizing this, the reformers Gertrude Jekyll and William Robinson invoked the garden of "nature" as a guiding hand. Colors must blend and a "wild" look be encouraged, preferably under a canopy of trees. Both Jekyll and Robinson were proponents of horticultural display, but they differed from other such proponents in that they thought of plants in relation to overall garden design. What this produced was the so-called wild garden, and, with the plant-explorer Reginald Farrer's help, the alpine garden. It should be noted that the English "wild" garden of this period was not devoted to native plants. Robinson's books included one on wild gardens and one on alpine flowers for English gardens, but his most influential work was *The English Flower Garden*, first published in 1883, which, by the time the author was eighty-seven, had gone through fourteen editions. The work contained Gertrude Jekyll's views on garden color, which she experimented with in her own garden, Munstead Wood, and in the gardens of other houses designed by Sir Edwin Lutyens:

> Should it not be remembered that in setting a garden we are painting a picture . . . a picture of hundreds of feet or yards instead of so many inches, painted with living flowers and seen by open daylight . . . so that to paint it rightly is a debt we owe to the beauty of the flowers and to the light of the sun; that the colours should be placed with careful forethought and deliberation, as a painter employs them on his picture, and not dropped on in lifeless dabs, as he has them on his palette?[34]

Francis Jekyll's memoir of "Aunt Bumps," as she was affectionately called, mentions that she retained throughout her long life a profound admiration for the French Impressionists. However, when the Impressionist Claude Monet made his own garden at Giverny, he massed his flowers in enormous confusion on one side of the house and concentrated on making his famous artificial water-lily pond on the other. Miss Jekyll was responsible for at least one garden in the United States, the Resor estate in Greenwich, Connecticut, and thought her own method of design would suit houses of the Colonial style, then being revived by the firm of McKim, Mead, and White.[35]

There ensued an architectural reaction to the "escapism" of the new gardening, as if European architects had awakened from the romantic dream of Arcadia. At the same time that William Robinson was advocating free-growing trees untouched by the hand of man, these architects were asking what was wrong with the self-assertive and confessed artificiality of topiary work, especially since it had been advocated by Alberti. In Germany, architects played with the idea of gardens as "outdoor rooms" of the house, supported by the influential writings of Muthesius and Schultze-Naumberg. Architect Reginald Blomfield's *The Formal Garden in England*, published in 1892, created a furor in England, asking as it did for a very different design from the landscape garden, which Blomfield considered an absurdity of bad taste. Robinson felt obliged to attack any return to the Renaissance-inspired art of gardens and put out a small book, *Garden Design and Architects' Gardens*, in which he abjured the "costly ugliness" of the system Blomfield sought to revive.[36] "We can have bits of rock alive with Alpine flowers," he proposed, "or pieces of lawn fringed with trees in their natural forms and as graceful as the Alpine lawns on the Jura." Mr. Blomfield writes nonsense, he said, and to clinch the argument he showed pictures of "vegetable sculpture"—"clipped trees in costly tubs" was his caption for an illustration of a handsome pleached allée in a country manor.

In spite of the fact the Blomfield's walled gardens with quincunxes of orchard trees and box-fringed plots of old-fashioned flowers were eminently suitable to the modest estates of the turn of the century (the National Trust's Hidcote Manor gardens may be taken as the type), most modernists would prefer the looseness of the landscape mode, so far into secessionism has architectural design plunged since the days of Frank Lloyd Wright. Yet an extraordinary revival of the Italian or "formal" garden took place in the years between 1890 and the late 1920s. It was to be found chiefly in America, coinciding with the excitement caused by the Renaissance revival in the architecture of that period. Edith Wharton, who was bored by her one visit to Munstead Wood, published in 1904 her influential *Italian Villas and Their Gardens*, with illustrations by Maxfield Parrish. The work of Charles Platt for Emma Lazarus at Cornish, New Hampshire, and at "Gwynn" on the lake at Cleveland, as well as the outlines of Edith Wharton's own garden at

Lenox, Massachusetts, are evidences of the best work of the early period. During this time even the Olmsted firm, so long associated with the picturesque, was making Italian gardens on Long Island and elsewhere, a tradition later carried on by Clarke and Rapuano. The most interesting public park in the Italian manner is Meridian Hill in Washington, D. C., with its cascade and reflecting pools. Later, in England, the architect Geoffrey Jellicoe, who has also written extensively on Italian gardens, was responsible for interesting formal gardens at Ditchley, Wisley (the water garden), and at Windsor. Gertrude Jekyll, who lived until the 1930s, saw in America "an almost passionate desire to make the Italian garden at all costs," but added, "I think the true Italian character is only suitable or completely possible in a corresponding climate such as that of California and others of the Southern States."[37] Certainly the most sumptuous of all the Italian gardens that remain to us is in Florida, the Villa Vizcaya (now the Dade County Museum), where the talented Diego Suarez, together with the architects Paul Chalfin and F. Burrall Hoffman, completed in 1921 the layout of its vistas and sculptured fountains against the blue waters of Biscayne Bay.

It remains for the poet to guide us back through labyrinthine paths to the true center of the maze.

"Tout le bizarre de l'homme, et ce qu'il y a en lui de vagabond, et d'égaré, sans doute pourrait-il tenir dans ces deux syllabes; jardin."[38]

The youthful poet Louis Aragon finds gardens strange and often ridiculous. The idea of gardens is as odd, he thinks, as the practice of blowing into brass trumpets. Little legendary paradises, he exclaims, you are the feminine element in nature, soft, curving, full of rounded places and declivities. Man forgets himself in gardens; he plays, casts off old ways, becomes emotional. The fairy tale, the primeval forest, even the belief in miracles is revealed here: "sous la piétre apparance démente de ces paysages faiblement inventés."[39] But man is pleased with his creation, "smiling gently beside the fuchsias."

All very well: one can find vanity in even the humblest surroundings. Vanity—Thackeray's "unseen spur"—has produced the highly-colored folk art of gardens that occasionally we see in unexpected places, unconsciously motivated.

GARDENS OF THE VILLA VIZCAYA ON BISCAYNE BAY. The architects were Paul Chaflin and F. Burrall Hoffman, and the landscape architect was Diego Suarez, who had also designed gardens in Florence. The whole estate was carved out of a natural hammock jungle. The great stone barge (opposite page) is a decorative breakwater designed by A. Sterling Calder (1870–1945). The estate was given by the heirs of James Deering, the owner and art collector, to become the Vizcaya-Dade County Art Museum. It is open to the public and supported in an appropriate manner by a non-profit citizens' group chartered by the state of Florida.

Aragon, then still in his Surrealist period, offers advice. People are afraid, he thinks, that if the garden is compartmentalized it will only look small. "Ah!" he says, "you have been taken in by the suburban approach. You have forgotten the taste for grandeur."[40] Abandon restraint. Don't listen to those who never thought of gardens as poems. Engrave your stones with philosophical maxims. Provide shady bosquets again. Remember the subtle advantages of the vista. Even the allure of the cascade. (He has been looking at a book of engravings by J. C. Krafft,

"standing at the brink of modern times," in which, significantly, gardens of the Anglo-Chinese taste predominate.[41])

A book of forty years ago included an explanation of the importance of science and specialization on garden design of the day.[42] Undoubtedly the combination of the "color gardeners" and horticultural "advance" has assisted the departure of any classical concept of landscape design. And has horticulture really advanced since the monks of the Abbey of Tournai in the time of Louis XIV exhibited their plants in "auricula theaters"? Scientifically, yes; but esthetically it would be unwise to accept current enthusiasms. There is, however, no doubt that interest in those species of the native flora that can be grown in gardens has increased the knowledge and awareness of natural phenomena and their role in the biosphere. Outcries against the disappearance of endangered species have resulted in new measures to protect flora and fauna in many countries. In the gardening world there will always be an interest in hybridization, but with this activity there now exists a parallel drive—to cherish older forms of plant life and preserve a far greater number of species, many of them once considered worthless or unsuitable for the garden. Interest in specialized forms of garden—ferneries, bog gardens, orchid gardens—and in the cultivation of single genera—primula, rhododendron, and iris among many others (we have already mentioned the pioneers of the rose)—provide evidence enough that the materials of gardening today have been expanded to provide a far greater corpus of knowledge on horticulture cum conservation than was the case a generation ago.

Apart from such material and cultural achievements, is the sense of an overall design completely lost to modern man? Let us acknowledge that, in acquiring that sense, there is no substitute for the direct emotional experience. And let us hope that on some garden pilgrimage, at dusk between dark hedges or against old walls, with a white glimpse of statuary at the end of a walk and the sound of water running softly somewhere near, the understanding of a man-made landscape heritage will begin.

TOWNSCAPE

Coming to Terms with Nature

Man who makes his home in the world has never been able to leave the landscape alone. Wherever he is, he finds himself adapting to or trying to conquer nature. With the trappings of civilization he sometimes improves his environment (one could cite certain cities in certain times), but more often the result is careless and haphazard. Sometimes he respects nature as a primeval force. Often, as a painter, he depicts nature, trying to capture a sense of its "incalculable detail," a refinement perfected by a Giorgione or a Titian.[1] He comes to admire nature's compositions for their own sake. He learns to appreciate the civilization of the ancients—and tourism is born in the Bay of Naples and the seven hills of Rome.

While we are now desperately trying to find ways of adapting to nature or working with it—a necessity thrust on us by mounting awareness of the population explosion, the many forms of pollution, uncontrolled technological expansion, the plundering of natural resources, and the expansion of cities—it has seldom been man's way of thinking to consider adaptation necessary, once problems of survival have been overcome. Those who have adapted perforce are nomadic communities, and hunters, and grazers, who depend entirely on nature's moods and cycles for their way of life, just as the delicate insect hides on the underside of a leaf when it rains. The Native American of the Atlantic coast, burning down trees and undergrowth to ease his way through the thickest forests, scarcely made a mark on nature; primitive societies were few in number compared with national groups today, and, anxious not to offend the gods, they were respectful of the deities' powers over man's rudimentary ways of making a living. Early societies might have caused a few patches of erosion or decimated a herd of wild beasts, but they did little damage to compare with our own ravages of the earth and sky. Today, those nations which live in poverty do less damage to nature than the richer nations, their chief crime being impoverishment of the soil. Max Nicholson reports that such East African tribes as the Masai adopted a more tolerant attitude toward their animal neighbors and competitors than did pastoralists of European origin, an admirable feature of African culture on which the world-famous national parks of East Africa largely rely.[2]

Man's acquired technological skills have modified and even created landscapes. In the small area of the British Isles, enclosure of common and arable lands, as well as large-scale agricultural schemes like the draining of the Fens, remade the English countryside in the space of a hundred years. Today the agricultural policies of the European Communities will change it still further, if the vanishing of small farms and orchards in northern France is any indication. The collective farms of Hungary have stamped a sweeping, open landscape pattern on what was recently a countryside of divergent holdings. We shall probably get used to the landscapes of modern agriculture, but, like modern architecture compared with the old, the new practices make the old farmsteads more rewarding visually and more desirable as incunabula. Already in the United States there is the Association of Living Historical Farms, designed to show farm life and techniques at specific periods in the country's past. One such farm in Iowa represents the agricultural world of 1840; there oxen are driven and shingles made by hand. We have had restored and reconstituted villages for some time, a measure demanded by a far-sighted few in an age losing touch with its traditions.

Historical restorations are of major importance in a rapidly urbanizing society; farming is not only disappearing in waves of suburban expansion, but is changing its character in many parts of the world—in parts of the American south, for instance, where cotton has moved west and is being replaced by grazing, and in South Asia, where dry rice cultivation has reduced the need for terracing and channeling in selected areas.

An accompaniment to all the changes, especially in the developed nations, is the desire to preserve "natural" scenery. Real wilderness being far from the urban centers, woods and forests nearby are receiving more attention from conservationists than formerly, as if in answer to Thoreau's plea that every town have a piece of wilderness nearby. Conservationists can take heart from the realization that "pure" nature seldom exists and that those few acres of scrappy woodland may be as near to the original state as they were before colonization. A generation brought up to believe in an ecological process leading to climax vegetation is now being told that it is false to think that before modern human disturbance the forest maintained itself in a stable climax condition.[3] Many of the scrubby forests we now have are apparently not very different from much earlier ones, an example of this being the revived forest areas that can be seen spreading across abandoned farmlands in the American east. While it would be going too far to suggest that the primeval forest is a romantic and nostalgic dream created by poets and painters who had seen large trees being felled in their favorite beauty spots, it appears to be true that in any given ecosystem the borderline between the artificial and the natural can be very arbitrary and that close parallels can be found between man's and nature's actions among the factors modifying forest ecology.

Attempts to conquer nature have accelerated in recent years. We have used chemistry to "improve" or destroy vast areas of the landscape, without achieving any better understanding of natural processes. The "green revolution" shows signs of backfiring. The science of biology itself, on which we rely for our knowledge of the natural world, is lacking in general laws, according to the physicist J. W. N. Sullivan, the theory of natural selection being useful for explaining many phenomena, but not all, while the Mendelian theory of inheritance "still encounters anomalies."[4] The subdivision of biology known as ecology has forged ahead; it now has some respectable methods of investigation, more sophisticated than those used in the late 1920s, when a course in plant ecology meant (to one student at least) a few pleasant Saturday morning rambles on Wisley Common. Sullivan, in his "approach to the unknown," concludes nonetheless that any profound change in our outlook on the physical universe will come about through the development of biology, and that while we have not yet seen the "oneness" of all nature, of which Teilhard de Chardin was so certain, we are moving toward abolishing distinctions between living and "dead" matter and a further synthesis among the sciences of mind, life, and earth.

Meanwhile, on another, more pragmatic plane, people attempt to classify landscapes (as distinct from landforms, which have received their share of attention from geologists). Some agencies, like the Commission on the Countryside,

HIGHWAY AS ENVIRONMENT. View of a gantry with periscope lens attached to a television camera which moves along a scale model to simulate an actual driving experience. Designed by Yale University city planners, its purpose was to enable the public and its officials to foresee the effects of a highway before it was built.

are concerned with every possible type of landscape. All sorts of subjective factors must enter into any scheme of classification, which surely must arouse misgivings among those who work only in mechanical or engineering systems. Only a few years ago a leading traffic engineering consultant refused to take part in a visual study of a proposed highway, because, he said, esthetic factors could not be measured. He has since changed his opinion, acknowledging that at least these factors should be given some weight. It is significant, too, that the United States Highway Research Board, since the passage of the Highway Beautification Act of

1965, has funded studies on the esthetic aspects of highway design for objectives other than that of traffic safety.[5]

Some others who have looked at highway location from outside the field of traffic engineering have arrived at systems of notation and evaluation which classify landscapes according to their physical and social "values." The studies of Lewis in Wisconsin and Ian McHarg in Pennsylvania are of this type. As McHarg explains on a road study: "The method . . . seeks to discern an alignment which least destroys existing social values, selects a physiologically suitable corridor, creates new and productive land uses and values, among which is the scenic experience of the traveller." Investigated are topography, flood plain, major bodies of water, historic sites, and so on; factors still not given adequate weight in the "least social cost" method include local opinion, politics, or basic economics. The choice of a route is further affected by the specific values given to the various factors involved in the survey. Nevertheless, these and other innovations, which include systems of visual notation, view "envelopes," pressure points, and other analytical aids, provide rudimentary guides for government functionaries. Nothing takes the place of the *insight* of truly humanistic observers who are moved by the forces of nature and who can invest even a humble forest trail with mythic and classical imagery.[6] Any humanistic discipline, if guided by imagination, can elucidate the landscape in new ways. Too detailed a classification can be a hindrance to imagination, but a broad-brush approach can illuminate. For instance, Robert Arvil (a nom-de-plume), in his book *Man and Environment*, devises a classification of "unities," or areas of land and water that embody all ecological types and at the same time the pressures calling for strong conservation measures. His examples are wetlands like the Florida Everglades, the East Anglian Broads, the Camargue in southern France, and various coastlines. Unities, or "entities," as one might prefer to call them, since the latter word implies distinctiveness and self-containment, have unique scenic values not always possessed by other forms of landscape. To enlarge Arvil's list, one might consider moorland, which the painter Lord Leighton found so fascinating. "The beauty of moorland," he wrote to his sister, "is that it has a particular poetry and impressiveness for *every* condition of atmosphere and weather." Heathland received its accolade when esteemed writers like Tennyson built their houses near Hindhead, with views over the Devil's Punchbowl, preserved with three square miles of common land by the National Trust since 1906.[7] Then there are certain river valleys that have received special attention from landscape connoisseurs, mountains (starting with Petrarch), hardwood forests (Burnham Beeches), and the maple-oak woods of Vermont, which are such a glory in October. Sometimes natural intrusions add greatly to the scenic interest of an "entity": Mont St. Michel in the racing tides off France's northwestern coast or Diamond Head off the southern coast of Martinique. The abruptness of dark cliffs rising out of the water in Lake Superior or the interface of the white cliffs of Dover on the English coast make lake- or seascape a special entity. Man-made intrusions in the view, however, are seldom compatible unless hallowed by custom or sentiment; the loss of the Catskill Mountain House, often painted by Cole and others of the Hudson River School, was a scenic loss, but a proposed motorway across Dartmoor or a bridge over Long Island Sound would bring severe damage to the prospect. A well-managed conservation and development project for an entity like the Lea Valley recreation scheme for Londoners, where the aim is to restore a degraded river (once praised by Isaac Walton) which has lost its capacity for self-renewal, is an admirable form of man's intervention, since it adds to inner suburbia a natural resource not usually found there.

Social Myths and Images

There is another kind of classification implicit in the mental attitudes of each generation toward landscape and scenery. Unconsciously in men's minds the forms take shape according to the beliefs and mythology of the moment. There was the landscape of the Golden Age, sung by Hesiod and Ovid, in which men lived in peace and innocence, which has been depicted in modern times by Thomas Cole's *Dream of Arcadia* or in the primitive painting *The Peaceable Kingdom* by Edward Hicks, wherein all the animals, wild and tame, lie side by side. As the art historian Heinrich Wölfflin pointed out, "Every generation sees in the world that which is congenial to it." The Romantics' search for the impossible led them to dreams of an age that they imagined as a pastoral state. The landscape suitable for Rousseau's natural man found a faithful copy in Ermenonville. For Wordsworth nature was a refuge, for the Improvers of his day, a bucolic world of sport and great estates. The world untouched by man is a more modern myth, although heralded by Romantics like Frederick Church in his paintings of Cotopaxi and other South American scenes. It is the wilderness experience of the naturalist, echoed in present-day attempts to set up communes in the forests and deserts of the American west or to live off the land in farming country.

If most of these landscapes were unattainable, they were nevertheless real in the minds of their creators. Similarly, the images that pursue us in our daily lives, although probably of a more mundane character, condition our views of city and country. The reality of our surroundings is in conflict with the ideal scenery we have been told about and shown in books and pictures; it is these latter images that are retained in the imagination of societies. A generation of Americans imagined Italian skies filled with creamy-white clouds just like those in the paintings of Maxfield Parrish, yet all the while the artist was drawing inspiration for cloud effects from the summer skies of Cornish, New Hampshire, where his studio was located.

Gathered images are important, whatever their source, for science tells us that visual experience is concerned with memory as well as with the art of seeing.[8] Apparently, visual perception can be identified with either pictorial memory or visual memory. Sir E. H. Gombrich[9] is of the opinion that the prime human instrument for communication remains the language, but he is not sure that this will always be the case, since the multiplication and manipulation of images have become so important in modern life. It seems obvious that the visual image will never supplant the exactitude of statement, say in a legal document, but it can certainly be more evocative (consider the impact of the sudden view or the spectacle of a forest fire).

In considering visual impressions it is necessary to know that people do not react uniformly to visual stimuli, thus there cannot be an identical group reaction to views or prospects. Highway engineers take this into account when designing roads, knowing that each driver displays individuality when interpreting his view of the environment. Age and physical condition affect his visual "intake." But since a journey along a highway consists of a series of stimuli to which a driver

Using a camera lucida, the English astronomer Sir J.F.W. Herschel made this pencil drawing in 1824. The subject is the Temple of Juno at Agrigento, Sicily.

reacts, some guidance can be found in discovering which objects are "most seen" (for we see a great deal with our marvelously sensitive eyes, but observe comparatively little). With the factor of speed involved, the motorist's view is largely restricted to a "visual envelope" or central arc of ten degrees each side of dead ahead. Travellers before the age of the automobile did not have the advantage of high-speed roads, but when they set out on foot or in a coach they were able to enjoy the landscape, like the poet Gray in a post chaise with his Claude glass reflecting every scene, or the Reverend William Gilpin with his sketchbook recording in Scotland the three parts of every view: Background, Off-Skip, and Foreground.[10] Compare them with today's driver on the freeway, required to travel at a certain speed with his eyes perforce fixed on the center strip and the right- or left-hand border of the road.

An eighteenth-century pocket-type camera obscura (Claude glass), much used then by travellers and topographers for recording landscapes.

Beyond the myth of freedom in travel (and related misconceptions) is the slow acceptance of reality when change has wrought its transformations of scenery or habitat. It is true that we have now come to think of Greece as a country of wild scenery, in contrast to that image implanted by classical archaeology, dominated by acres of Parian marble and bathed in the calm light of ancient philosophy, but we still have odd ideas about landscapes much nearer home. One of these is the image of town and country as discrete entities, which was only true in certain now-remote civilizations, and in its physical manifestations can now be found only in a few medieval relics, in France, say, or Spain. Certainly the urban influence now continues throughout all distances, as the demographers tell us, and few parts of the world are without some of its manifestations. The increasing importance of wilderness to modern man is an echo of this condition. The new realists (branded by technocrats as "soft-headed dreamers") are the environmentalists, spurred by the deterioration, if not the "disappearance," of the countryside and now involved in political battles of great magnitude. The old mistrust of the city lingers, however; it takes as its text Cowper's famous line in *The Task*, "God made the country and man made the town." Time was when the city was considered a part of the natural order of things, and a view of New York harbor with its sailing ships was considered as beautiful as Niagara Falls, yet an emphasis on its present deficiencies makes the city appear ugly. This is having its effect on every manifestation of our culture.

Going further back, we can find a more balanced view of the city among the philosophers, especially in Aristotle's *Politics*:

> The proof that the state is a creation of nature and prior to the individual is that the individual, when isolated, is not self-sufficing; and therefore he is like a part in relation to the whole.[11]

When Cain builds the first city, it is a substitute for the Garden of Eden. City and country. Neither exists without the other.

Aristotle described the city thus:

> When several villages are united in a single, complete community, large

enough to be nearly or quite self-sufficing, the state comes into existence, originating in the bare needs of life, and continuing in existence for the sake of a good life. And therefore, if the earlier forms of society are natural, so is the state, for it is the end of them, and the nature of a thing is its end. . . . Hence it is evident that the state is a creation of nature.[12]

Although Aristotle made the famous statement that man is a political animal, he did not assume that the city-state was a creation of politics. He thought of the city as growing naturally and run like a household, with an agricultural or pastoral democracy as the best form of democratic government. The flocks of the pastoralists move freely about in the city and in the agora, he observed, and even in the outlying districts the cattle-herders mingle together and can readily come to the assembly.

This elegant concept of an ideal community—*organic* is probably the best descriptive term—bears little relation to what we see around us. The argument that the individual in the state exists to perform his assigned or natural function, especially as described by Plato, has been challenged by those skeptical of present-day environmentalist thinking who find an over-extension of the organic metaphor in the use of laws of the natural environment as a moral code for man. In particular, it is felt by some planners that the "conservatism" which they find innate in the ecological approach is inimical to the solution of the pressing problems of the city. However, the argument that societies and states are not organisms but rather voluntary associations of human beings is quite unsatisfactory when applied to the phenomenon of today's city.[13]

The modern city would have seemed unnatural to Aristotle, if only because of its size. Its complexity would probably not have worried him, but he would have found the lack of communication between its individuals and its groups disturbing. He would have understood our preoccupation with health and safety in the city (these were foremost with him, too) but it would have been hard for him to understand why the flocks were not in the agora and why there were so few flowers, trees, and fountains.

The relationship of man to nature in the city has usually been discussed in terms of facilities offered and recreation afforded. Nature is alien in the city and its bounty grudgingly provided.

No one would doubt that man is at the center of urban affairs or that these are activities proper to man alone, but now that the study of natural systems has shown that man and the city are part of ecological phenomena having a direct bearing on all life on earth, the whole question of man's urban existence and the kind of city he builds must be looked at in a new way, in terms of the environmental revolution. We are living in a fool's paradise of reckless energy and resource consumption.

The concept of the city as a specialized independent unit is new enough for its effects to remain unexamined and old enough to be accepted as inevitable. One may date as one chooses the time when art was separated from religion, business from culture, and the practical from the esthetic. The city which Aristotle regarded as a natural phenomenon and in which the Platonic Academy of Florence planted its orchard became in successive stages a mechanism and a market. The last it had always been, but not to the exclusion of beauty and grace. Hence the violent reactions of nineteenth-century reformers who tried to turn the city back into the small town via the garden city, and the despair of some present-day intellectuals who find in the modern metropolis nothing but degradation and evil. The persistence of the notion that man is born good into surroundings that are corrupt, a Romantic fallacy, accounts for much that has misled the modern mind.

The idea that the city is part of the natural order is long since gone, together with the once-accepted belief that man and the other animals are all a part of God's creation. Newer beliefs, like that of evolution, are difficult to apply; the city may have its own laws of growth and decay, but they are man-made and not the result of random selection. Man himself, however, is not exempt from natural laws, although he tends to use the earth to his own advantage, secure in the false belief that technology will somehow rescue him from his mistakes.

It is common knowledge now that we live in a finite world in which the per capita share of the world's goods is steadily decreasing. This closed life system is the biosphere, "a thin veneer encasing the globe," just a few miles up or down in vertical measurement. The bulk of mankind is inexorably bound to this ecosystem, and man alone of all the animals is able to use the earth and oceans correctly as well as to his own ends.

The point here is: if we were to consider the city as part of the natural order, we would have better reason for cherishing it. Meanwhile, considering the city as an artifact is important for "landscape through the eye" and vital for preservation efforts. The prospect of the city, its situation, its silhouette, its various parts—the street, the square, the groups of buildings—all these components provide aspects of community appearance. Jefferson remarked that surroundings that reflect "a low, commonplace or eccentric taste" have a debasing and dehumanizing effect upon the spirit. Since city and countryside are now merging into one human habitat we must pay special attention to all parts of it as "landscape" and not isolate the term by thinking of it as applicable only to wild or rural terrain.

Threats and Intrusions

Equally applicable to town and country are two diminishers of the cultural heritage: intrusion and destruction, both of which in their differing ways can affect the appreciation of urban and rural scenery. It should be understood that many segments of society are involved in these depredations and that there are constant surprises demanding quick action, especially in the case of demolition of structures; also it must be pointed out that while many private and public bodies dedicated to preservation and development of the cultural heritage exist, the public or governmental side can be as culpable as any individual or private corporation in the spoliation of the landscape.

"Nowadays only about seven Wren spires can be picked out from London Bridge, subject of course to whatever huge block rears up next week."[14] The writer thinks a sense of prospect is needed, citing as a pioneer example a Committee for Preserving Open a View of the Tower and Spire of Saint Bride's Church in Fleet Street of 1825. Present-day city fathers and developers lack a feeling for setting, and they prefer something new over something old. One particular horror was the post–World War II plan for the area around Saint Paul's Cathedral; who would not have preferred the Lutyens plan of 1942?[15] "Nobody wanted enough to preserve that close vertical slice of St. Paul's, ground to cross, once to be seen along the old

Cannon Alley from Paternoster Row." And what about the view of the west front, now eaten into by a projecting piece of glass—not, one would think, a fitting approach for the cortege of any of Britain's heroes. When the old London Building Act, which restricted the height of buildings to eighty feet, was removed in 1956, permissiveness led to changes in the skyline. True, subsequent regulations designated some areas as "sensitive" and "inappropriate" for tall buildings, but the word *forbidden* does not appear in these regulations, and many choice views have been invaded.[16] When H. L. Mencken,[17] visiting London in 1926, asked Beverley Nichols, "What the devil are you doing to London? Do you want to make it into another New York?" he was talking about new buildings in the Strand and across the Thames that *conformed* to the height limitation. *Aegrescit medendo*, the disorder today increases with the remedy. Now Saint Paul's is hemmed in from almost every side. Across the Atlantic, Richardson's Trinity Church in Boston, an American landmark if ever there was one, has been intruded on by an expensive piece of "glassville," a building plagued with construction troubles. To add insult to injury, Trinity has been faced with a garden of concrete. Private and public interests have combined in the "New Boston" to create many similar horrors, especially since the coming of urban redevelopment in the 1960s. And now we hear of a twenty-story hotel next to the Forbidden City in Peking.

Paris has fared somewhat better, the result of severe restrictions on new building in the central zone of protection. Many are the oil companies who would like to have built skyscrapers (*gratte-ciels*) along the Champs Elysees or in the path of other famous views. But "the sense of prospect" does not extend far enough, it seems. Many Parisians were shocked when distant tall buildings suddenly appeared to rise at the end of residential streets, although they were being built at Montparnasse and La Defense; worst of all, the vista from the Voie Triomphale to the Arc de Triomphe was marred by a slab-like structure, erected in the La Defense region, that could be clearly discerned through the Arc.

Smaller cities have taken the intruding blow for various reasons. Padua, wanting to be a second Milan, has allowed tall buildings to spoil its formerly arcaded streets. Willemstad in the Netherlands Antilles now has a hotel built in the midst of its harbor fort. Aswan, on one of the most beautiful stretches of the Nile (and a

An old photograph showing the traditional Nile sailing boats (feluccas), taken in the vicinity of Aswan, a winter resort and traditionally the southern limit of Upper Egypt. Here the river curves and is full of islands, affording much of interest for travellers. One of the islands, once owned by Lord Kitchener, is now a botanical garden. A tall new hotel dominates Elephantine Island, once famous as the site of the Nilometer, an ancient device which recorded the rise and fall of the stream, now controlled by the Aswan Dam.

famous winter resort), is dominated by a hotel tower on the Elephantine Island. Cannes has become a sprawling mass of high-rise apartment houses, while Lugano, on a physically restricted terrain, has crowded them into the central business district. But not all resorts have permitted the past to be destroyed. Little Portofino allows no new building; that is rare. Rothenburg has skillfully patched its war damage and hidden its petrol pumps in recessed courtyards. Salzburg has very strict regulations on building additions in the old city. Most such regulations in Europe have been in force for some time; in the United States, San Francisco has begun to see the light (after a rash of tall buildings has shut it out) and is considering height restrictions as well as a ban on tall buildings in certain parts of town. The tradition is there: it was the City of the Golden Gate that stopped a freeway in mid-air some years ago and began instead to build a new rapid transit system.

Pioneers of Scenic Research

If Thoreau wanted the wilderness preserved from man and Marsh the depredations of mankind curbed, it remained for the age of finance capital to produce individuals who sought a marriage of man and nature through good design. Such a one was the German architect Paul Schultze-Naumburg (1869–1949), a progressive designer of houses and gardens before World War I, who became an antimodernist during the Weimar Republic, attacking modern architecture's impermanence and shoddiness. His later career, under the shadow of Naziism, should not obscure his earlier contributions; indeed, many pre-Nazi land-use laws stemming from half a century ago are part of the present-day West German legal code. One has only to leaf through the hundreds of photographs in his *Die Gestaltung der Landschaft durch den Menschen* (1916)[18] to realize that most of our current problems, from billboards to wetland preservation, are being solved. Schultze-Naumburg was a misguided idealist who finally lost all intellectual respectability, but he can be seen to have welcomed the "Blut und Boden" ideology as a fulfillment of his commitment to "Heimatschutz" and "Heimatkunst" and as a rejection of the industrial-commercial world which he had come to hate for its destruction of traditional values.

Schultze-Naumburg was one of the first artists to classify landscapes by type and detail, as well as to delve into the esthetics of industrial development, for which the neoclassical architect Karl Friedrich Schinkel had provided models so long before. He avers in his three-volume work that man has the power to enhance, damage, or destroy nature, and goes on to propose that anything man-made should be a harmonious part of the landscape, an organic entity with nature. This symbiosis once existed, he explains, but was undone in the second half of the nineteenth century when economic considerations won out over an understanding of nature's beauty. The only remaining untouched areas are the high mountains, parts of the seashore, and heaths. He traces the development of man-made objects in the landscape, starting with roads and paths, which were once harmonious with nature because they had more or less to conform to the terrain. Modern roads, he observes, consist of straight lines connected by curves with a short radius, a condition which was corrected by German highway engineers some years later when they came to build the *autobahn*.

Writing about the effect of husbandry, including forestry, Schultze-Naumberg objects to forests planted in geometrical squares, too many conifers, and untidy cutting. Their edges should be shaped, he says. "If a flower dare grow, a school class comes along and rips it out by the roots for a 'demonstration.' " He notes that the grove, once a cult place for worship and sacrifice, exists no longer. (It was revived by the Nazi youth for their outings.) He likes the old alleys of trees, now being cut down,[19] as well as the planting of individual specimens, like the planting in village centers of linden trees, around which all public activities revolve. He deplores the cutting down of hedges on farm property and admires the pattern of vineyards on German hillsides. All this is illustrated by well-composed photographs.

Waxing lyrical over geological formations ("Every landscape has its own individuality, like a musical composition expressing itself through the dynamics of its elements"), he cites the unwelcome effects of quarrying, singling out big companies especially for taking down whole mountains. He maintains that an "anti-disfiguration law" is needed, "as it already exists for monuments and advertising signs." As for power plants, they are committing what might be called a theft from everybody. Dams can be esthetically pleasing or the opposite. One must weigh any newly created landscape values against those that are lost. The bold technician who masters all these natural forces must want to unite his work with the beauty of the world.

Continuing, Schultze-Naumberg says that there is not much natural water left. Swamps are thought to be unhealthy; the only dissenter from this view is the hunter of waterfowl. Contemporary bridges are not landmarks for their communities, nor works of art; they have no relation to their environment. Any industrial building constructed between 1860 and 1905 is usually ugly, a situation that Krupp realized and tried to change with his own industrial architecture.

On the other hand, human settlements can be the most desirable objects in the landscape, especially if one is Robinson Crusoe or an inhabitant of a sparsely settled country like Canada. They are the focal points to which all ways lead. But no rules can be set up as to how a single building shall be placed in the landscape. A building on a lonely mountain top will make it seem still lonelier. Coming into an old city one is led to the center of community life in a way that does not happen in more modern settlements. An analysis follows showing settlement situations—on a hillside, in a hollow, and so on. Farms, villages, and small towns are all part of the landscape, from a distance. When they are approached, parts of the landscape become framed by buildings. A hill town is also seen as an entity. Or consider Tubingen, built on one slope and seen from an opposite slope.

Modern cities possess confused, vague traits. They look as if a giant's child had split a box of white dice over the landscape. This picture complements political and social conditions which have become more complicated and ill-defined. As for village life, industry and its workers' housing colonies are taking it over.

What is the most egregious structure in the open landscape? The hotel. It simply does not adapt to the landscape picture. Schultze-Naumburg refers to "hotel pests." Hotels do not grow out of the ground like ruins, "which touch the soul of man." Ruins have shapes which have taken on a degree of softness. They cannot be improved in any way. Worse than tearing them down is trying to restore them or changing them into beer restaurants.

Schultze-Naumburg concludes by avowing that what we now call "improvement" owes mainly to the creation of gardens and parks, which are only suitable to certain natural settings. Much of England, obviously, provides such settings, but an essentially park landscape can become monotonous. Germany, he warns, should not lose its character in this way. The Deutscher Bund Heimatschutz helps to preserve her beauty, but its intention is not to isolate landscape from civilization (as has been done in the United States in the case of parks like Yellowstone National Park). An all-round harmonious civilization is the aim. Some laws are already in existence to enforce this. Above all, financial gain to the individual should never win over public advantage (a concept that was built into modern zoning). So ends the last volume.

Certainly the recognition of entities is an important part of any way of looking at nature, or of giving the view an overall rating. A landscape is not featureless, and within its horizon are elements which contribute to diversity, texture, and clarity. An ecological scientist would also consider its health, judging this by the quality of vegetative cover and other clues. For the landscape connoisseur, matters of detail, contrast, and scale may be important, while color acts to strengthen the visual impression. So also does a geometric pattern, natural or man-made, either as a point of reference or a part of the total pattern. One must, to educate and strengthen his impression of land, seek out esthetic quality in the landscape. People go to art museums with just this intention. Why not to the out-of-doors?

The same humanistic approach can be made to cities, with a slightly different emphasis. Instead of paying only perfunctory attention to a city's skyline or overall view, one can focus closely on single elements of the city. Many are the ways this has been applied to individual buildings since the rise of architectural criticism in the nineteenth century, but the urban ensemble has received less attention. Brinckmann, Sitte, and Zucker have examined town squares, the last-named especially having evolved a rather simple but man-oriented classification of squares as dominated, nuclear, closed, grouped, and amorphous.

Schultze-Naumburg adopted in his *Staedtebau: Herausgegeben vom Kunstwart* (Munich, 1906) certain viewing-points in city streets, open, closed, curving, and so forth; he then photographed them and reproduced the scene in plan and thumbnail sketches, showing the lines of sight and describing the esthetic impact of the view.[20] He also illustrated steps, walls, textures, and surfaces, showing how they add scale and interest, using examples mostly from such central European cities as Prague, Jena, Pirna, Danzig, and Basel. This method of analysis has been elaborated over the years, especially as photographic methods have grown increasingly sophisticated. One very lavishly illustrated work on city analysis is *Italian Townscape*, by Ivor de Wolfe (a pen-name for H. de C. Hastings, publisher of the English *Architectural Review*). His urban categories include Invitation,

Convexity, Precipitation, Personality, Action and Inaction, and Remoteness—an indication of how romantic his approach is. Ingenious as the townscape observers are (there have been many followers of the *Architectural Review* method of analysis), their combined efforts tend to reinforce the picturesque effect rather than to re-establish the lost principles of urban design so sadly lacking in the vocabulary of modern secessionism.

In recent years attempts have been made by professional architects, landscape architects, behavioral scientists, and others to classify landscapes in terms of scenic values. These efforts have been spurred in part by world highway building programs, recreational activities in the countryside, and so on. They may be concerned with scenic road potentials, containment of views, or consideration of disruptive elements. Sometimes they have been involved with river valley esthetics. Their obsession with labels rivals that of the eighteenth-century landscape estheticians Price and Knight, whose concern with the origins of taste and varieties of pictorial composition nevertheless led those rivals down very different esthetic paths. The present-day analysts of landscape values tend to use semi-scientific classifications—terms like *segregation*, *gradation*, *edge definition*, *biological corridors*, and *setting units*—and whereas it may be good practice to draw attention to perceived phenomena by relating it to known examples of a similar nature, the whole question of quality somehow eludes this labelling process except on a very limited scale.

The flood tide of landscape analysis has nearly reached us. None of these technical experts are *vedutisti*—an occupation which will probably always remain the best method of investigation. Some physical geographers have lately entered the field and have made interesting contributions. One of these is Jay Appleton, whose theory is that man responds to landscape through primitive instincts, resulting in an animal need for "refuge" followed by observation from the safety of "refuge" toward the "prospect." The refuge-prospect idea is cogently argued, but one has to bend many landscape experiences to make them conform to the theory. Thus the author of *The Experience of Landscape* finds no fundamental difference in landscape perception among the fox hunter, the deerstalker, the mountaineer, the fell walker, the poet, or the painter.[21]

By using "doctored" photographic examples, Paul Schultze-Naumberg was able to present his ideas of landscape improvement, in this case concealing the effects of industrialization by tree planting and other means.

Let us consider what UNESCO had to say concerning "the values of the past and the beauties of nature":

The following are considered to be the major threats:
a. Urban expansion and renewal projects.
b. Injudicious modifications and repair of individual and historic buildings.
c. The construction or alteration of highways.
d. The construction of dams.
e. The construction of pipelines and of electricity power and transmission lines.
f. Farming operations, including deep ploughing, drainage and irrigation operations, the clearing and leveling of land, and afforestation.

g. Works required by the growth of industry and the technological progress of industrialized societies.[22]

In this list, farming would seem to be the least destructive activity. Who has not admired green pastures and arable fields? Yet farming can be destructive. Man as pastoralist, according to Max Nicholson, is responsible for the destruction of forest cover and the transformation of forest to steppe and steppe to desert, or, in the case of the denudation of the Scottish highlands, to what Sir Frank Fraser Darling has called a "wet desert." Pasture erosion can be found in the uplands of the South Island of New Zealand, that paradise of lush grassland, but more spectacular erosion could be found in the southern United States when cotton dominated the export market there. Now, not only have the crops been varied but conservation of the soil by better cultivation methods has been introduced, prompted by the TVA yardstick in the 1930s. One cannot view with complacency any landscape that has been badly treated by man; changes in landscape brought about by natural causes can be equally grim, like the devastation of forests in the northeastern United States by the 1938 hurricane, but nature usually heals its own wounds eventually, whereas man can render it infertile or remove entirely its source of growth—the soil. An everyday example to be seen near the big cities is the extraction of gravel for road building or the disappearance of whole hillsides into the rock crusher. The fringes of the city, which used to be the place for farming or the hunting of marsh birds, are nowadays, unless protected, subject to horrendous amounts of dumping, excavating, and other land uses unwanted in the central city. The edge of the city was once a favorite site for the artist to set up his easel when he was making a topographical sketch. In more recent times it was a place for the amusement park at the end of the trolley line, the site of trotting races in Harlem, or of boating on the Seine outside Paris. The mass production of automobiles changed all that. Only now are cities trying to make their rivers pure and their harbors safe again for swimming; there are still tremendous pressures to use them for dumping industrial waste and sewage.

> Ah, happy hills! ah, pleasing shade!
>   Ah, fields beloved in vain!
> Where once my careless childhood stray'd,
>   A stranger yet to pain . . .
>
> [Thomas Gray, "Ode on a Distant Prospect of Eton College"]

These hills and fields are still there, happy because longstanding patronage has ensured that they have not gone to the rock crusher or the garbage dump. Happy, too, because the country in which they are found, like others of northwestern Europe, has a tradition of land management which takes amenity into account.

Town and City Views

Since the town and city form a denser part of the total landscape, they deserve a closer look, especially at their centers, where everybody tends to gravitate at one time or another and where the greatest opportunities exist for civic art and composition.

There may be several centers, depending upon the size of the settlement, but a distinguishing mark will usually be some attempt at order or monumentality. A town will have a marketplace, but it will also have a church or churches and a square or green, a town hall, banks, and a post office. These may all be grouped together, they may be separated in different parts of town, or they may line a street. Their relation to topography—a temple to the gods was often on the highest hill in ancient times, as it is today in modern cities like Liverpool and Washington, D.C.—their architectural quality, their associations—people will regret the loss of Les Halles in Paris until they come to enjoy the public garden which takes the place of the destroyed market—their ceremonial function: all these things help to comprise the attraction a city center holds.

Where monumentality appears, be it in street, square, or single public building, there one will usually find an important view, from the vista of the Mall in Washington or in New Delhi, to the apse of Saint Peter's, that extraordinary exercise of Michelangelo's in *terribilitá*. No doubt the greatest concentration of public architecture in history could once be found in the Roman and Imperial fora, overlooked by the Palatine and Capitoline hills. The administrative center of Rome is still on the last-named, but nowadays there are other centers as well. The president lives on the Esquiline, there is the Via Veneto of the great hotels, and who has not lingered on the Spanish Steps? The pope has a little city of his own, the railway station has its plaza, and the great suburbs to the north and west have substantial centers, too. Mussolini's ill-fated Città EUR exposition (Esposizione Universale Roma) in the south is now the nucleus of a thousand offices. Although no longer the center of the known world, Cosmopolis has dressed up its old bones in new clothes and still outclasses most other great cities in its scenic attractions.

Metropolitan improvement dates from about the mid-eighteenth century, when cities began to grow in importance (London, shortly after 1800, became the first city to reach over a million in population). This movement accounts for much in our civic tradition, producing the avenues, malls, bridges, residential squares,

THE FAIR AND ITS SUCCESSOR, THE MONUMENT GARDEN AT PADUA. A neoclassic transformation of the Prato della Valle (opposite page), once the ancient Roman heart of the city. Its pre-1790 appearance was recorded in Canaletto's *The Fairground* (above).

terraces, and mammoth building complexes which have added so much to the ambience of cities, as well as the lighting and paving acts which made them more liveable. The idea of improvement soon caught on in countries outside England, and although a city like Paris or Budapest would have its own priorities and methods of financing the work, metropolitan improvement, together with railway building, became a mark of nineteenth-century cities everywhere, demanding flotation of municipal bonds and new concepts of running municipal affairs. The results might vary in appearance, since the nineteenth century was notable for successive waves of architectural fashion, but what was done remains constant in the municipal *vade mecum*—street widening, park systems, governmental centers, and so on. Tentatively, metropolitan improvement began to embrace housing, as in the Metropolitan Houseless Poor Act of 1864 in Queen Victoria's reign,

but "improvement" here was slow in coming. One cannot find much to admire in the grudging gestures that were made in working-class housing until quite recently.

A prototype combining several of the new elements can be found in the Padua of about 1775. Many of the city's improvements were inaugurated by Andrea Memmo, then *provveditore*, who was a leading figure of the Venetian Enlightenment. Since Padua has suffered in war and peace, it has to be imagined nowadays what the city looked like when it still had arcaded streets before one side or both of the arched walkways were removed for street widening. But the town retains unique features in addition to its artistic treasures inside the Carmine and elsewhere. There is the charming Orto Botanico and Memmo's town planning scheme, combining commercial functions with "a didactic program of sculpture," which used to be called the Prato della Valle. Originally the center of the Roman town, and formerly an ancient meadow of irregular shape used for fairs, it was transformed into an oval green space planted with trees and surrounded by a formal canal. From beneath the arching branches, statues of bygone Padovans and academics stare out at the passerby. Earlier statues would have been of gods and mythological figures. It was still unusual to commemorate persons, and the proposal to do so created a furor in Padua at the time. The statues, which, aside from a couple of works by Canova, are not renowned, mostly have the place to themselves, except for the annual June fair, when the large open space around is noisy with horse races and vendors of *bagattelle*. There is a modern loggia (1861) across the way used by the judges, and a Renaissance church hiding in another corner of the irregular piazza, which is now named after Vittorio Emanuele Secondo. Altogether it is one of the most singular and serene examples of open-space planning to be found anywhere; it seems to follow Alberti's advice in the fifth book of *De Re Aedificatori*: "Colonnades open to the sky ought to be embellished with green things, for walking in the air is very healthy" and particularly so "in the refined and rarified air that comes from green plants."[23]

For an eighteenth-century small town center seen as civic design, nothing can serve so well as the King's Square in Spanish Town, Jamaica, the old capital. On one side is the Palladian King's House itself, now merely a facade, but still the

King's Square in Spanish Town, the old capital of Jamaica, surrounded by fine buildings. This photograph was taken from the balcony of the House of Assembly (c. 1762) looking toward the Rodney Memorial, a classical "temple" containing a statue of the admiral in Roman costume by the English sculptor John Bacon.

most imposing building in the view. Built circa 1762, it was followed in the 1780s by the arcaded Rodney Memorial[24] on the west side of the square. On the other two sides are the municipal archives and the courthouse. Now the object of a restoration program, this symbolic center of a government that once existed delights the eye and allows the mind to contemplate past celebrations, victories, and other national occasions.

There is greenery in King's Square; it is subordinate, as is usual in neoclassic

ALDINE SQUARE, CHICAGO. Residential squares, such as Hudson Square in New York (now destroyed) and Grammercy Park, could once be found in some midwestern cities, echoing their prototypes in England.

town plans, a contrast to the overemphasis on lawns and shrubs one sees in many modern schemes. It is not enough to base planning on amorphous greenery, as the promoters of Charles Center in Baltimore professed to do. "By adding open space as a new element," they advise in a brochure for this renewal project, "the psychological refocussing of Downtown can have physical expression. Green fingers . . . further pedestrian malls and tree-lined streets . . . form the visual structure of a revitalized Downtown." Any project in which open space "forms the visual structure" is bound to remain structureless and marked by the hand of the rationalist, which has blighted so much modern civic design.

There are countless excellent examples to include in a list of preferred urban scenic views, but near the top (and gigantic spatially as compared with little King's Square, which yet appears spacious in itself) is the Palace Square in Leningrad. Everywhere in that city one is aware of civic art and design.

Inside, it is a city of malachite, gold, and marble (*vide* the restored Saint Isaac's Cathedral) and of extravagant conceits in unfamiliar materials. Where else except in these environs could one see a room done in amber? (Alas, it must be imagined, since it was dismantled and carried off by the Nazis and has never been found.) Where else can one still find an eighteenth-century roof garden? (In the Little Hermitage, with a seven-foot depth of soil to support large trees, and squirrels, pheasants, and peacocks brought in during the tsarist regime to amuse the royal children. Nowadays it is full of workers and their families resting tired feet after going through the three hundred rooms of the state museum.)

Where else a pair of rostral columns, formerly serving as lighthouses on the Neva and even today alight with flames in times of celebration? Where else so many monuments to revolution? Perhaps in the United States?

Although it is customary for the books on planning history to dwell on the boldness of Leningrad's early plan, it is the ensembles of the eighteenth and early nineteenth centuries which give the city its monumental character, the genius of the plan resting mainly in the placing of the complexes on *both* sides of the river and running a goosefoot of streets from the admiralty site. But it is the detailed composition of the squares and gardens and parks which excites the imagination. The Fortress of Peter and Paul, the Stock Exchange, the Winter Garden with its statues and *fer forgé* grillwork in black and gold on the Neva Embankment—all contribute in their variety to the classical theme.

Peter the Great brought Carlo Rastrelli, the renowned sculptor, to the city; it was Rastrelli's son Bartolomeo who built the Winter Palace in 1764. He and De La Mothe are the most famous names of that period in Russia, while Andei Voronikhin, Quarenghi, and Carlo Rossi were the leading architects of the first third of the nineteenth century.

It is Rossi who is especially impressive for his civic designs. It was he who shaped the Palace Square opposite Rastrelli's masterpiece. Born in 1775, he died in Saint Petersburg in 1849. His mother was a prima ballerina in the theater at

PALACE SQUARE, LENINGRAD.

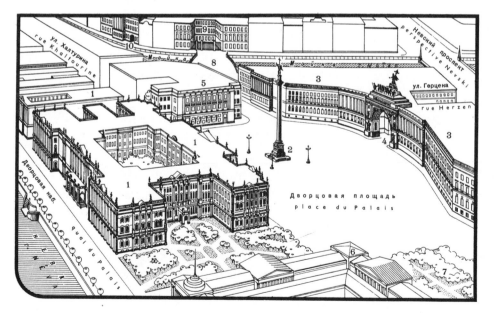

Saint Petersburg. Rossi could design anything, from a pair of vases in the antique manner for the mother empress to continuous facades half a mile long, so that it was no trouble to complete the square when the government bought up the houses to the south of the palace in the early nineteenth century. He constructed the immense ellipse of the General Staff Headquarters and the Ministry of Foreign Affairs to enclose the almost twenty acres of the square. In the center of the curve is the triumphal arch which marks the victories of the 1812 war. Surmounting it is a chariot and six horses, with arms and weapons of war, weighing sixteen tons. Climbing to the top, Rossi answered Nicholas I, who had questioned the safety of the arch when completed, "If it falls I am ready to go down with it."

Beyond the arch is Herzen Street, partly designed by Rossi. It comes into the square from an angle, laid out along the Pulkovo Meridian, so that at astronomical noon its houses have no shadows.

In the center of the square is the Alexander Column of 1834, a massive granite affair, held by its own weight, which all the bombs and shells falling in the nine hundred days of the Leningrad siege failed to dislodge. At the top is an angel, whose face is a likeness of the tsar.

The visitor will not fail to see the Square of the Arts, especially if he goes to the Maly Theater of Opera and Ballet, whose architect worked from Rossi's sketches. In fact, Rossi planned the whole square, and its generous proportions reflect his skills at the very first glance. Dominating the ensemble is the imposing Mikhail Palace (1825), built for the youngest son of Paul I, with its great forecourt and grille. It became the Russian State Museum under Alexander III and is now the State Museum of Russian Art.

A feature of the interior of the museum is the Hall of White Columns, which has murals depicting scenes of the Trojan War. The hall was so admired in its day that the tsar ordered a model of it to be made and presented to George IV. The model maker was rewarded by the king with a gold medal and commissioned to do wood carving in England.

The square owes its success to the uniform cornice line, the proportions of its fenestration, and the continuous facade treatment of a diversity of buildings, with very subtle differences in the design of window frames, doorways, and other details. After being damaged during World War II, the facade of a school on the eastern side was brought into line with the rest, and the garden in the center of the square replanned to afford a better view of the Russian State Museum. The garden contains a statue of Pushkin by Mikhail Anikushin (1957); as is the case at all memorials to the poet in the Soviet Union, offerings of fresh flowers can usually be found at its base.

These and many other fine examples of civic art were obviously created with forethought. Less obviously, they are still there for us to enjoy because they have been regarded with special care and attention, guarded by law, and tended by dedicated personnel. Even a shabby, run-down building, if it has architectural or historical interest, or if it is a part of some worthwhile civic ensemble or handsome street, is better than a hole in the ground. This concept of looking at a *complex* as worthy of preservation, including structures of lesser interest if they are important in the view, has been accepted by the international preservation movement. The fight to keep a district intact has been won often enough to provide precedents for all countries to follow. Nevertheless, there are constant dangers. It is not enough to keep an inventory of buildings to be preserved: that is only the first step, and it must be followed by preservation laws with teeth in them. "You know when towns are demolished it just happens," wrote a keen observer of her modern European environment, " . . . comes the bulldozer and it is all over in a trice."[25]

Sometimes the impending danger is slower in advancing, as the following example of the resolution of an urban conflict shows.

The Vieux Carré in New Orleans is much more than the birthplace of jazz. It is architecturally important in the New World, with its successive French, Spanish, and British builders, and even more so in its nineteenth-century American dress, which is mostly what we see today. Jackson Square, for example, was completed then. Buildings by Latrobe and other well-known architects have been preserved, largely through the benevolent but firm regulations of the Vieux Carré Commission, one of the two oldest historic district organizations in the United States. These regulations have been invoked against many proposed demolitions, and they have likewise been instrumental in keeping the construction of hotels and

The Louisiana State Bank, in the Vieux Carré, New Orleans, designed by Benjamin Henry Latrobe, one of the architects of the United States Capitol. The building is now occupied by an antique shop.

restaurants (for this is an economically important tourist mecca) at a scale which does not disrupt the skyline.

Jackson Square, the former Place d'Arms, with its handsome cathedral, Cabildo, and the flanking Pontalba "apartments," is in the National Register of Historic Places, as is also the old Ursuline Convent, which looks as if it had come straight out of some fine French provincial town. The old United States Mint is nearby. The whole district has a cachet quite rare in North American urban life

A view of the cathedral in the Vieux Carré from the center of Jackson Square, showing wrought iron furniture.

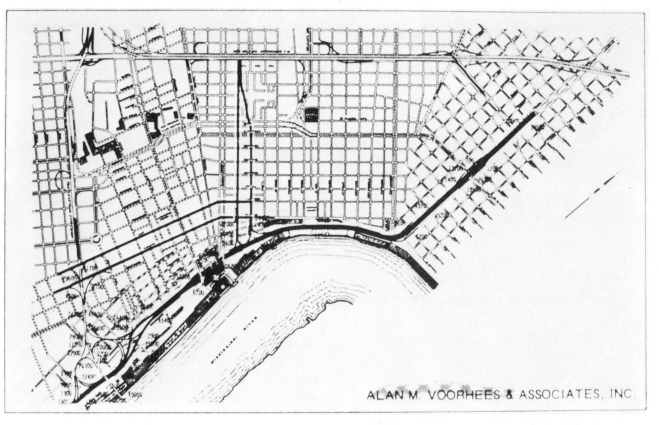

Plan showing route of the proposed Elysian Fields Expressway.

and is cherished by the public-spirited Orleanaise. But in 1965 a most important event took place, largely unnoticed except by professional preservationists. The entire historic district, comprising all of the eighteenth-century, 300-foot-square blocks, was declared eligible for designation as a national historic landmark because of its "national significance in American history and architecture." With the passage the following year of the Historic Preservation Act, the district became eligible for protection, just when the worst threat to its viability became imminent.

A highway along the riverfront and almost touching Jackson Square had been proposed at least since 1944, when the New York public administrator Robert Moses had been called in as a consultant and had made a recommendation to this effect. By now the project had been magnified into a six-lane interstate facility to be known as the Riverfront-Elysian Fields Expressway. The cost of the 3.4 mile section through the Vieux Carré was set at about 31 million dollars if the road were to be elevated; if it were to be depressed, running between Jackson Square and the Mississippi River, it would cost an additional 12.4 million dollars. This expensive alternative had been put forward by the engineers when local and national controversy over the building of the expressway had reached its height; in the meantime a ground-level scheme in the same location had been approved by the city council in a vote of 4 to 3. There were rumors that some very powerful people in the state and national governments were in favor of this route. In the financing of any of the schemes, it should be realized that the federal government, as in the case of other "links" in the interstate system, would bear most of the cost of construction, and that the state of Louisiana and the city of New Orleans would be very unlikely to "go it alone."

The national Department of Transportation was now constrained to take into account the effect of the proposed highway on National Register property, which in this case was the entire French Quarter. The National Register entered a variety of opinions. "One of the needs this road is supposed to fill is to take heavy traffic out of the historic district. The bulk of the traffic in the Vieux Carré, except during brief rush hours, is made up of visitors and local residents, none of whom have great need for a new highway." Again, "Much has been said about the relative costs involved in these schemes. From a preservation standpoint the cost of the road cannot be measured against the loss in esthetic and historical values caused by the construction. If the engineers' main concern is cost, there is [another] alternative—building no road." And again, "Motorists can now bypass the Vieux Carré if they desire to do so. This proposed highway, because of the turns that have to be made to skirt the Vieux Carré and the river, would appear to save only about two thirds of a mile provided that the motorist is going from the intersection of Interstate 10 and Elysian Fields to the Greater New Orleans Bridge. Otherwise, it will be the long way round."

Both sides had done their homework well, which was brought to the attention of the Advisory Council on Historic Preservation when it was called in spring 1969 to a lengthy public meeting in Washington where the sides presented their cases. The council then spent three days on the site and subsequently made its recommendation, which was essentially adverse to the construction of the highway, although it considered the depressed scheme to be the only acceptable solution if an expressway were finally to be built. It is believed that this action finally sealed the fate of the expressway. In any case, a depressed version would have been bitterly fought by the Port Authority because it would have disrupted wharves and shipping facilities. However, the Federal Highway Administration had recommended the depressed version, and its officials were taken aback when the Secretary of Transportation overruled the administration by refusing to grant the necessary federal funds because the highway would have "seriously impaired the historic quality of New Orleans' famed French Quarter." He also held that the disruptive effects of the highway, its excessive costs, and the construction hazards it posed to the Mississippi River levee that protects the entire city made it unacceptable. The *New York Times* was of the opinion that the current public outcry against the disruptive effects of federal highways in inner-city neighborhoods had weighed heavily in the decision. There was something else. The members of the advisory council, besides the private citizens appointed by the president of the United States, included the secretary himself and six other cabinet officers. Further, when the council votes, the department heads concerned are a party to the recommendations made. Under these circumstances a national council on historic preservation in which the departments concerned are constrained to take into account the effect upon cultural property listed in the national protective inventory of all federal, federally assisted, or licensed undertaking can be influential indeed.[26]

Preservation by legal ordinance or financial assistance is only a first step—allowing the fabric to stay. How it is to be maintained, developed, used, and lived in then becomes of immediate importance.

The French term *mettre en valeur*, often used in connection with land improvement and now adopted by the preservation fraternity in their international conferences, can be roughly translated as "to enhance," implying a conscious upgrading of a preserved district or community to give it new life and activity. The

REPLACEMENT FOR LES HALLES. Design for the new park in the French manner which conceals elaborate underground service and sports facilities on the site of Les Halles. To the east may be seen the Centre National d'Art et de Culture Georges Pompidou, to the west is the circular Bourse du Commerce. The church of Saint Eustache lies to the north. The designer is the Catalan architect Ricardo Bofill.

French "showpiece" (though by no means the only example in France) is the district in Paris known as the Marais.

The Marais is Old France—with underground parking. It was always celebrated and has become fashionable again, but fashionable in a different way from the sixteenth arrondissement or the Ile Saint Louis. It is a great mixture of things, which adds to its charm. Most of the streets are medieval, and it is easy to see where they have been modernized (widened) under the law of Louis Phillipe, the bourgeois king, by the sudden breaks and juts in the streetscape. You can walk into the courtyard of an old inn, or up the staircase of an *hôtel* that is being restored, to find workers taking off the false ceiling put up by a little nineteenth-century manufacturing concern to reveal a seventeenth-century vision of the gods at play in heavenly perspective. The greatest French architects and artists of the classical tradition worked in the Marais, and there is something interesting at every turn.

"Marisium qui jacet inter Parisius at Montem Martirum" it was in the twelfth century—the marsh which is situated between Paris and Montmartre. Stagnant water, rushes, little islands, with rivulets descending from the hills, occupied only in summer by basket weavers, brickmakers, and mendicants. There are still a great many small workshops devoted to a variety of hand technologies, as well as artists' studios, tango dance halls, and religious houses. Every Paris riot has had its repercussions there, with obstructions put up in the narrow streets to be fiercely defended by the inhabitants.

Roman roads crossed the marsh, the present rue Saint Martin and another, lying under the rue Saint Antoine. Unhappily, this was not the end of the transportation story.

No quarter of Paris was ever constructed as a museum, and the city has announced that no sterile preservation methods will be employed anywhere. But the Marais *is* a kind of museum, albeit a very lively one, and it is called today the "ville musée." It has a famous square as well as all those grand palaces and intimate townhouses. And it has the national archives of France and the Carnavalet.

Not only are houses and palaces being restored, but *jardins à la française* as well. Often these gardens lie over the parking garages, while trellis work rises above to screen unsightly walls. A certain amount of screening is inevitable since earlier demolitions, new schools built by the city under the influence of Le Corbusier, and street widening have left scars that nobody wants to see.

There will be no more street widening. Baron Haussmann is dead at last. Take his proposed extension of the rue Etienne Marcel, which starts at the Place des Victoires, to cut through the Marais as far as the *grands boulevards*. Even after Haussmann fell into disfavor, and until very recently, the Marais was never safe from intrusions of this kind. Luckily, there was not always money to expedite them, beginning with the day the city of Paris agreed to pay back some of the huge debt that Haussmann had run up with the Credit Foncier.[27] But bits and pieces of widening were done along the proposed route in 1884, 1906, 1924, and 1937, especially at corners where the new street was to cross other thoroughfares. Preservation groups were inactive or powerless. The Old Paris Committee, to which the project was referred, actually accepted the city's proposal to finish the whole job in 1932 (regretfully, it said, but in recognition of the "incontestible utility" of the scheme). Houses were demolished and activity continued until the fateful year of 1939.

After the war and the suffering it brought, preservation of France's heritage suddenly became desirable to many more people, and the conservation of whole groups of buildings was demanded. The long-projected Haussmann plan—the extension of the rue Etienne Marcel–rue aux Ours, with its widening of existing streets and cutting through *îlots*—would have destroyed the Hotel Guenegaud (by Mansart) and the hotel d'Hallwyl by Ledoux, restoration of which had already begun. This was the catalytic step. The city council effectively came to the rescue by making the whole of the Marais a protected zone in 1956. In 1962 came the "Malraux Law" for all France, with its crucial provision of funds for restoration; it was applied to the Marais by decree in 1965. One can now walk down the whole length of the once-projected traffic artery where the *hôtels* have been handsomely restored, remembering that a hundred years of "planning" for a new thoroughfare had doomed them to be swept away in the wake of Haussmannization. The scale is kept, the pedestrian is catered to, and the lover of townscapes has his just reward.

The detailed town planning on which the revitalization of the Marais is based allows for surveys of public opinion as well as the delineation of main and subsidiary traffic routes and the relation of mass and scale in new building to the old. If some buildings are deteriorated beyond repair, they may be removed; the plan specifies whether or not they should be replaced by buildings that will "fit in." Minor buildings provide the "connecting tissue" but they must respect the regulations on appearance, color, openings, materials, and roof slope specified in the architectural schedule.[28]

The problem of modern buildings in old settings has been complicated in most countries by the insistence of their architects in using outworn rationalist forms and listening to "the whisperings of privacy" rather than submitting to group responsibility. A town predominantly Baroque in its architecture, Buda (of Budapest), picturesquely rising above the Danube, has successfully avoided such mistaken ideas in its rebuilding after bomb damage, but other "museum towns" have not fared so well. In Nuremberg, as it was explained to me in the office of the Stadtbauarchitekt, there was no state law on reconstruction as in many other West German towns, and the city had promulgated its own regulations. "We have tried to keep the 'face' of the town, in spite of the demands of modern commerce. New building has to be in the spirit of the old." Tall buildings cannot be built in the old center of the city, although there is a quite prominent glass-and-steel tower not far from the art museum.

If, on the other hand, a building is not too far deteriorated, it is built as it was. Dürer's house and a number of landmarks have been completely restored. The town hall has a new wing on one side of its courtyard with larger windows, and quantities of steel strengthen the old masonry walls.

On the north side of the old city especially, where there were so many of the old, typical Nuremberg roofs, the rebuilding must employ the original tiles, or tiles of the same color and same materials must be used on the exterior. The original roof height must be kept, and even the old windows. In several buildings, however, much more glass can be noted than was to be found in the original buildings.

LIMITED PRESERVATION. The Peller-Haus at the north end of the Egidienplatz in Nuremberg was the finest late Renaissance building (1605) in the city, with an interior three-sided arcaded courtyard. After war damage this interior was restored, with a modern front facing the square. More usual is the practice in the United States of restoring the facade and gutting the interior for modern "improvements." Neither method is correct.

At first the rule was firm in retaining the old window openings. Later, shopkeepers complained that they wanted bigger windows "to get more light" and the rule was relaxed.

In the Egidienplatz, formerly one of the most striking architectural ensembles, a decision was made not to rebuild the *pièce de résistance*, a patrician townhouse of the Renaissance period. The excuse was that the style was so florid and covered with ornament that it would have been too expensive to reconstruct. Only the foundation was left, to a height of a few feet above the street. The interior courtyard *was* restored, forming the nucleus of a new state library and archives, and a modern facade erected on the old foundation in the front. The contrast between the bland glass facade and the Renaissance court behind, with its elaborate stairway and beautifully carved new stonework, is very odd and definitely disturbing. When one visits the Dürer House, surely one of the finest private house museums to be found in Europe, and experiences vividly the feel of another century's life and manners, it seems a pity that this other example of high bourgeois culture could not have been sympathetically brought back to us. The Germans are masters at historically correct restoration. If the price was high, was it actually more to pay than the false bargain of modern architecture at any price?

Where there is no problem of a new-old relationship, urban composition ironically enough may be more difficult nowadays since designers do not understand classical principles and, when starting from scratch in a cleared "renewal area," have no basis on which to proceed. Since the designers of Lincoln Center have stated that the Main Plaza (Avery Fisher Hall, New York State Theater, Metropolitan Opera) was inspired by Michelangelo's Campidoglio in Rome, it may be instructive to compare the two spaces. First, the Metropolitan *does* dominate the space, but the directional pull is not strong; the opera house does not provide the focal point that the Palace of the Senators, with its central tower, does: it is architecture without mass and without surface shadows, since the glass front is not set far enough back from the arches. Instead the front is made very tall, which does nothing to improve the proportions of the plaza, the width of which in relation to the height of the opera is in the ratio of 1:3.5 plus, and rather excessive.

The result suggests that the designers had tried to make the contained space of the plaza appear smaller than it is, but that was surely not the intention. The three large buildings could have been treated to enlarge the apparent size (with steps outside rather than inside), but instead they are set down like puddings on a platter, bland, smooth, and bare of ornament, so that the space appears dwarfed. In the two flanking buildings on the Campidoglio the sculptor artfully makes the rather

LINCOLN CENTER, NEW YORK CITY.

low facades seem higher and nearer in scale to the Palace of the Senators by introducing giant pilasters, whereas in the New York State Theater the architect merely tried to make his frontal columns seem to taper by incising converging lines in the travertine, an effect which can barely be seen from ten feet away. The device of repeating a module of bay units around the plaza fails because this attempt at echoing a colonnade leads nowhere.

By contrast, the asymmetrical North Plaza, loosely organized around a giant sculpture by Henry Moore, seems more sympathetic because it does not attempt an unobtainable effect. In trying to be monumental, modern architecture is bound to fail, producing monsters instead of magestic images.

In surveying these few examples of townscape we can see that although every solution must be different in scope and scale, accepting the urban realities and economic conditions of its time, certain standards can be set up against which to measure results. One of these would be the proper siting of buildings in the sense of taking advantage of topography and exercising kindness toward one's neighbors. Another would be a knowledge of the canons of classical architecture, without which one cannot fashion a proper doorway or an architrave, as well as knowledge of the scale of a pattern of paving or a window opening. Included here must be a recognition of the values of proportion, not only in buildings but in streets and squares. Above all there must be an awareness of what the city means to people. In this way senseless or greedy destruction of esthetic values can be avoided and the amenities of Aristotle's "natural" city be achieved.

LANDSCAPE AND SCENIC PRESERVATION

Scenic preservation is of even more recent origin than the conservation of cities (itself only a generation old), but it has become alarmingly necessary in the wake of population increase and technological change.

Although the contemplation of mountain and valley scenery has been celebrated since the eighteenth century, its preservation was deemed unnecessary except in game reservations (nowadays wildlife areas), national or state parks, monuments, seashores and recreation grounds. In the early days, if views were preserved they were usually commercialized, as in the case of Virginia's Natural Bridge or Switzerland's Falls of the Rhine.

Significantly, it was a painter who called early for a national park, "a *Nation's Park*, containing man and beast, in all the wild and freshness of their nature's beauty." This was George Catlin (1796–1872), who suggested in the mid-eighteen thirties that a great strip of the plains country be preserved by an agency of the United States government as a home for the Native Americans and their buffaloes. His paintings are a reminder of these peoples and their pursuits, but a park on the scale of this grand conception would not have been a popular project in those days.

In the United States, Hot Springs National Reservation was the first "national" reservation to be set aside (1832), but it was not scenically important since the springs themselves were in the midst of a fair-sized town. The Yosemite Valley became a sort of state park in 1864, while in 1872 the Yellowstone became the first national park in what was to become the remarkable United States system. Successive presidents added acreage to that system, and dedicated secretaries of the interior like Harold Ickes fought for its expansion.[1] The latest United Nations list of the world's national parks gives 1205 in 80 countries, most of them on the North American continent.

The national parks are nearly always possessed of scenic attractions, but now that no part of the natural or man-made landscape is safe from depredation or intrusion, additional policies and ingenuity are necessary to insure that the public

FALLS OF THE RHINE, SCHAFFHAUSEN, SWITZERLAND. The greatest waterfall in Europe was an early tourist attraction and the subject of paintings by Turner and other famous artists. Seen from below it is largely unspoiled.

interest is served. The Areas of Outstanding Natural Beauty in Britain are examples of the new thinking. The principle of inalienability was incorporated into the British National Trust Act of 1907; only by resort to Parliament can it be abrogated.

It would be erroneous to give the impression that scenic values can be captured for posterity as easily as snapshots or landscape sketches. Their boundaries are not easy to delineate satisfactorily, just as historic or conservation districts of cities

ENCROACHING ON A FAMOUS VIEW. Seen from above, the waterfall at Schaffhausen appears rather different, given the urban sprawl on the far side.

have proved awkward to limit in many cases, showing the need for discontinuous historic districts when widely-separated parts of the community are to be covered. If a line must be drawn, where does one draw it? At the ridge line of the surrounding hills? That is one of the easiest cases. What if there are no abrupt rises in the topography? A common phrase now used internationally is "within the viewing area." This may ensure that all areas in view are protected, but hidden dangers may lurk beyond. When the United States Congress drew a boundary of a quarter of a mile upslope from the center of California's Redwood Creek to protect a thick forest of the world's tallest trees, this was deemed sufficient by the politicians. However, clear-cut logging operations further up the hillsides subsequently created serious erosion problems on the lower slopes, causing some of the giant redwoods to topple over into the stream and fish-bearing pools to silt up. One of the most awe-inspiring natural areas in the world was thus endangered, ecologically and visually.[2]

It is important to take as much land into consideration as possible. This fact of life is leading to measures of protection taken nationwide. A writer on Switzerland notes: "Chair-lift terminals, mountain roads and railways, huts, tall tele-communication masts, concrete markers, pipelines and penstocks, dams and spillways, pylons and power-lines are prominent features of some of the world's grandest scenery." The Swiss are of course conscious of all this and are passing a landscape protection law.[3] In Vermont, where the tops of mountains are equally threatened by the promoters of ski-lifts and an urbanite influx generally, a statewide land-use law has been effective in preventing much further desecration.[4] Florida has also taken measures to protect an even more fragile water-based environment.

Many of the views we wish to protect have been modified by man's activities and form part of the cultural patrimony of a nation. A threat to the site of a famous battle, where the contours of the land have been softened by time, can be taken as seriously as the danger to some outstanding natural beauty spot. Let us consider an example.

Saratoga has been called one of the decisive battles in world history since it turned the tide of the American Revolution. Burgoyne's surrender on October 17,

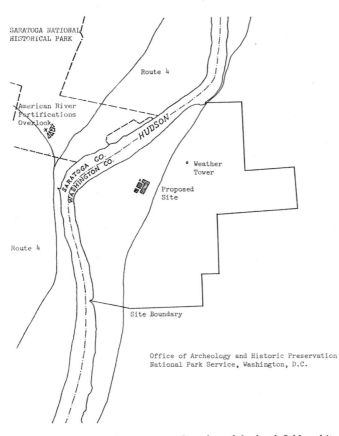

SARATOGA NATIONAL BATTLEFIELD. Site plan of the battlefield and its
view across the Hudson River.

1777, when the depleted British army of 6,000 men stacked its arms along the west
bank of the Hudson in defeat, encouraged a hesitant France to intervene openly
on the side of the rebels. Formerly a state park, the immediate site of the battle,
on bluffs overlooking the great river, is now a national historical park, administered by the National Park Service, which is "dedicated to conserving the natural,
historical and recreational places of the United States for the benefit and inspiration of all the people." The Park Service was alarmed in 1968 when a private
utilities company proposed to install a nuclear power generating plant on the
opposite and very rural side of the Hudson, in the foreground of the magnificent
view from the redoubts. Other local bodies and private individuals were protesting

BEFORE AND AFTER. The top photograph shows the view from the Saratoga battlefield across the Hudson River. In the bottom photograph an approximation of the proposed nuclear power plant has been sketched in.

the plant, largely on the grounds of thermal discharge effects on the waters and on the atmosphere, but there were adverse comments on the design of the plant itself, which included a 169-foot-high reactor and a possible 350- to 400-foot-high emission stack, the whole occupying a cubic footage roughly equivalent to that of the Library of Congress in Washington (although scarcely comparable to that edifice in architectural merit). One of the opposers, the Hudson River Valley Commission, publicized the fact that the power company had already begun excavations for the plant, although no license to build had been received from the United States Atomic Energy Commission.

At this point the Historic Preservation Act of 1966 was invoked. As we have seen, the act requires that an opportunity to "comment" be afforded the Advisory Council on Historic Preservation on federally licensed private undertakings affecting historical property listed in the National Register. The advisory council met at the site and decided that the effects of the proposed plant were "sufficiently adverse" to make their consideration important in the Atomic Energy Commission's decision whether to issue a permit. Like other United States governmental bodies, the Atomic Energy Commission is required by law to take into account the effect of proposed licenses or funding of new construction on places like the Saratoga National Historical Park. It did not issue a license for the undertaking on the proposed and already occupied site.

The arguments of the council raised some interesting esthetic points. They established the principle that historical properties should always be considered in relationship to their environment, not as isolated entities. This was very much along the lines of comparable ICOMOS-UNESCO resolutions. These international bodies have recognized the fact that the immediate environment often includes properties in which unsympathetic intrusions can damage the appreciation of a monument. In the case of Saratoga, the government does not own the entire area in which battle manuevers took place. Furthermore, the site is much as it was in the eighteenth century, and the view from the redoubts, taking in several miles of agricultural and forest scenery, is unspoiled. It was argued that feasible alternative sites for the nuclear plant had been under consideration, while the battlefield site would always have to remain where it was. In more recent experience, environmental impact has become a mandatory consideration in many states and in federal undertakings for every kind of large-scale development, indicating that cultural values are being given more importance in the landscape than heretofore. In the important case of Saratoga, the paramount issue was the preservation of a view central to the understanding of how a battle was fought. A letter written by the power company states that plans for the proposed nuclear power plant opposite the battlefield "were shelved due to anticipated delays in construction." It also indicates that the company is not seeking any sites for plants, nuclear or otherwise, on the scenic Hudson River. However, other companies have plans for various plants further south along its banks.

Private development on private land is subject to more restrictions than formerly. One must remember that in the United States, a country long dedicated to the proposition that individual or corporate ownership of land in fee simple is the most desirable kind of proprietorship, controls over other than the public domain were rare until fifty years ago. Similarly, public agencies are being subjected to stronger controls than before. A clause in the Environmental Protection Act, for instance, requires environmental impact studies to be made on any major project in which federal funds are involved. Since these funds are always involved in interstate highways, atomic power plants, and other public utilities, many wetlands and woodlands have been saved by the invocation of this clause by aroused citizen groups and wildlife societies.

The ominous effect of strip mining is well known in the United States, particularly in the eastern and central states, where the acreage affected has been over four times as great as that in the Federal Republic of Germany and the German Democratic Republic combined. In Europe it is freely acknowledged that afforestation projects in areas affected by bituminous stripping have been more impressive in the United States than elsewhere.[5] While it is difficult to convert strip-mined areas into field crop or meadowland, forms of woodland can quickly be established in parts of the country which have moderate rainfall, especially by using pioneer trees such as the black locust, a leguminous tree which does not need humus in the soil in order to survive. Land intended for pasture can have cover crops consisting of vetches like *Coronilla varia* or *Medicago sativa*, which likewise do not need humus. Recently, the European black and gray alders which seed and spread rapidly have been found useful as shelter trees for the more permanent species which follow them.

Reclamation of this kind is accomplished most successfully on relatively level or gently undulating land. In mountainous country, where the coal seams lie horizontally to the slopes, major problems are involved. To work these seams, the new giant earth-moving equipment casts rocks, trees, and earth down the flanks of the mountain, causing silt to fill the streams below. On the uphill side of the trench, the "high wall" can rise to eighty feet or more. The "big screws" follow along, boring for remaining coal deposits, a method which is estimated to recover only 30 percent of the rest. Where the exposed sulphur-bearing coal is left behind, the surface water draining from it has been found to kill many forms of aquatic life in the lakes and trout streams.[6] Concern over this type of mineral extraction and over the recent extension of strip mining to the Indian and government coal lands of the west has caused the Congress to pass a new bill which stipulates that the mining companies fill in the high-wall excavations wherever they occur.

Apologists for the externalities of surface mining have sometimes claimed that the results after "restoration" will be an improvement on the original appearance of the land. Others have admitted to finding beauty in the by-products of the operation. "In some cases, such as Central Illinois, the barren spoil banks (by creating scenery contrasting with the beautiful monotony of the cornfields) can represent a highly desirable and interesting feature of the landscape" was a remark made at a natural beauty conference at the White House in 1965. In general, however, it would be better to adopt the cautionary attitude to tampering with original conditions held by historic preservationists, whose motto is "It is better to preserve than repair, better to repair than restore, better to restore than to reconstruct."[7] Surface mining should never take place in areas of outstanding natural beauty, for reclamation there cannot achieve verisimilitude or even settle for harmlessness. Nor should it, in a time of national and international food shortages, be allowed to conflict with agricultural production.

Much ingenuity has been displayed in finding adaptive uses for mined areas. After treatment they have provided flat land for sports fields or contoured land for

STRIP MINING RECLAMATION.

golf courses. They may also serve as a depository for objectionable by-products of the city. A five-acre strip-mined coal pit near Pittsburgh has been transformed into a stocked game preserve, with layers of processed municipal waste sandwiched between layers of soil. This was compacted by hydraulic ram to prevent any possible spontaneous combustion, and a twelve-foot layer of soil was placed on top. This reserve was developed by a coal company. The cost to the city for waste disposal was reduced to $6.85 per ton from the $25 per ton, which would have been the cost of incineration, with its attendant effects on air quality.[8] In the state of Indiana, where professional reclamation staffs are employed by the mining industry acting in cooperation with government agencies, major recreational facilities have been created in a state park and a state forest on land largely disturbed by strip mining. In a 175-square-mile anthracite area of Pennsylvania, a power company contracted with the forest service to map spoil areas requiring tree cover, including screening unsightly views from main roads. Much of the planting was done by volunteers from youth groups.[9] Some of the trees were moved onto the sites by new transplanting equipment. The new town of Columbia, Maryland, has relocated thousands of trees moved both when dormant and even coming into leaf by a safe and easy method of moving grown specimens which utilizes a patented transplanting bucket. This method has been used by highway departments for tree moving on the site of superhighways and by the Chicago parks department.

All this ingenuity and more is needed to combat the ravages of strip mining, sand and gravel excavation, and rock-crushing operations for the supply of coal, building materials, and highway construction. In the states in which strip mining is carried on, the total acreage affected by highway construction was over fifty times that of the mining area, according to a survey conducted by the TVA a few years ago. The machines now used in strip-mining will move 210 tons of earth every 55 seconds. The biggest machines are now taller than Niagara Falls, as high as the Golden Gate Bridge, and eight traffic lanes wide. Beside them, the little tree transplanting bucket seems puny indeed, but, although it cannot perform as fast, the results of its work add a certain grace to the denuded landscape and provide esthetic satisfactions as well as the practical ones of preventing erosion and affording cover for wildlife.

One of the worst eyesores affecting scenic preservation policy is present-day waste disposal. Great efforts to recycle solid waste are being made by governments and private firms. Important decisions loom as the nation's waste products are tapped for re-use; for instance, paper can be recycled and used as paper, but it can also be treated and used as a much-needed source of fuel. The proper allocation of such resources becomes critical in times of national shortage of raw materials, a fact with far-reaching implications for import-export policy as well as for simple domestic consumption. Apart from these important considerations, it is quite possible to dispose of solid waste effectively if land is available, but the "burn or bury" philosophy of the past is being abandoned in favor of the recovery of most that is thrown away. It is now possible to recover about 80 percent of municipal solid waste; the technology of recycling is already in existence and markets for its products are being created.

Sanitary landfill, as the most acceptable method of disposal is called, will presumably always continue to be used, if only in the case of residue which cannot be recycled. This method replaces the old town dump, which was often on fire or swarming with rats. At present, solid waste disposal is a very serious problem in country towns where unspoiled landscape is an important desideratum, because the amount of land available for this purpose is diminishing. It is no longer possible (and was never condonable) to dump garbage into marshes or over the side of cliffs; sites have to be selected with care and paid for with local funds. Sanitary methods are required in most communities. Earth-moving equipment must be bought and prescribed methods of banking, trenching, and compacting employed, lest the leachates escape and contaminate the ground water. Eventually, when the landfill is completed, it can be planted and even built upon. Compacted trash has been used to create ski slopes in flat country; a sanitary hill has been created at Virginia Beach, where it is known locally as Mount Trashmore. New York City is considering building an island of trash in the bay, with concrete walls to protect slippage; this would be an improvement on present methods of towing garbage out on barges and dumping it in the Atlantic.

Apart from solid waste in the form of garbage and trash, the problem of automobile, washing machine, and refrigerator disposal looms large in scenic preservation. These items, known as consumer durables, reach obsolescence earlier in this country than they do in other parts of the world. The abandoned automobile has become a feature of American fields, roadsides, city streets, back alleys, streams, vacant lots, and woodlands. One can even see the occasional private airplane discarded and rusting near the many country airfields. There would not be so many of these eyesores if the cost of moving them to a scrapyard were not so prohibitive to former owners and scrap-metal merchants. There are about eight thousand auto wreckers in the United States; they handle six million cars a year. On their premises used cars are purchased and dismantled for the main purpose of salvaging usable parts, which go to the automotive rebuilders. This process is familiarly known as "cannibalizing." For instance, the city of Chicago delivers and sells to scrap metal firms approximately 35,000 abandoned cars a year. After cannibalization, the rest is sold as scrap. Inevitably, the wrecker's yards, ranging from two to eight, or at most thirty, acres in size, are full of rusting bodies, the average age of which is seven years—full, that is, unless the bodies have been compacted by machine. But car-flatteners and portable balers are still expensive for the average scrap-metal merchant, who has traditionally been a small businessman, although there is now a tendency toward a concentration of power in the industry. In many communities, local ordinances require fencing or screening these yards from public view, but, as in the case of so many other industrial processes, the best results for landscape appearance consist in speeding up the flow of scrap to the steel mills and further improvement of scrap-processing equipment and reusable parts, the latter to enable cars to last longer on the road. Substantial new outlets for automobile and other metal scrap are being made possible by governmental experimentation with systems of concentrating and reducing low-grade iron ores that so far have not been used commercially. The metal would, after processing, reenter the steel-making cycle at the initial stage. The pickup and disposal of abandoned cars may also be accelerated in the new systems of general waste disposal.

Affecting scenic values are other forms of decay which are the result of changing technology or obsolescence. At the White House natural beauty conference I made suggestions for the decaying urban waterfronts of the United States, noting that consolidation was in order and citing the example of San Francisco Bay, which is ringed with obsolete wharves, and where one marginal berthing facility of sufficient width could accommodate all the oceangoing ships ever to be found at one time in those waters. I advocated retention of some of the piers in New York, especially the Chelsea Piers designed by the turn-of-the-century architect Whitney Warren, which are handsome examples of industrial architecture and which could provide recreational facilities as well as examples of historic preservation. And I recommended that urban waterfront districts be established to insure that these important parts of cities should become a cultural resource and that scenic zones should be established there on the lines of item 16 in UNESCO's "Recommendations concerning the Safeguarding of the Beauty and Character of Landscapes and Sites" (December 11, 1962). In these zones, permission would have to be obtained for new installations, including highways, which often pre-empt the best sites on waterfront land.[10]

A slow and difficult form of reclamation is being applied to the nation's dead and dying lakes, where eutrophication and man-introduced agents, more poisonous, have destroyed living creatures and plants. These agents, which may or may not be deleterious in other situations, range from mercury to gypsum to phosphatic detergents to oil waste. They are by-products of industrializing societies, and although ingenious methods have been devised for recycling many of them before they reach the water, the lakes nearest to centers of population have all suffered in one way or another from contamination, either directly or by means of the entering rivers.

One of the earliest attempts to protect the waters of a lake occurred in the 1890s when Chicago created a sanitary district far beyond its borders and entrusted this new authority with the creation of a sanitary and ship canal which reversed the flow of the Chicago River to prevent it from polluting Lake Michigan, the source of the city's water supply.[11] This industrial river thereafter flowed out of the lake instead of into it, at the same time providing a navigation channel and making Chicago's swimmers safe from pollution along the miles of sandy beaches with which the metropolis is endowed. A 1973 plan for the lakefront aims to acquire all the remaining private land along the thirty miles of beaches to maintain their continuous character for the public.

It was not possible for the city of Cleveland to do the same thing with the rushing Cuyahoga River, the surface of which burst into flame when its floating industrial waste was one day ignited. The Cuyahoga flows into Lake Erie, which is shallower than Lake Michigan. Among other industrial cities on the borders of Lake Erie are Toledo and Buffalo. There has been a severe deterioration of the waters, massive fish kills, and a drastic curtailment of the lake's recreational potential. At the Lake Erie Congress, held in 1971 under the auspices of the Great Lakes Research Institute and other organizations, the following suggestions for further research and action were made: (1) Improved methods of treating wastes and effluents; (2) Interaction of the lake's physical, chemical, and biological systems with emphasis on the natural self-healing process; (3) Quantitative analysis of trace metals, pesticides, and other toxic compounds in the lake; (4) Useful recycling; (5) More effective water management policy, including means for controlling fluctuation of the lake levels. It was also recommended that a cost-benefit study be made of the ongoing cleanup process.[12]

Apart from the more noxious wastes, eutrophication is a common condition, one which can occur far from an industrial area or visible human habitation. Eutrophication consists in the favoring of certain species of algae by the introduction of phosphates or other nutrients, changing the body of water from an oligotrophic system which supports plant life to a eutrophic condition which supports much more. Eutrophy is an aging process in lakes; in nature many thousands of years will pass before a lake becomes a swamp and eventually dry ground, but human intervention may speed up the process disastrously.[13]

The United States Environmental Protection Agency identified the "problem" lakes of the country in 1971, describing some of the variations in their health and the methods of attack being used to combat the changes in water quality. The largest natural lake in Connecticut, for instance, which is very small compared with Lakes Michigan and Erie (only 915 acres in extent and a mere 25 feet in maximum depth), but very important for recreation and wildlife, has been treated for eutrophication once a year for six years with copper sulphate to study the effect of artificial destratification by aeration. Anticipated in future work on this lake is a method which does not use this chemical, to which fish are allergic. In another lake nearby the water level has been lowered in winter for the past three years to kill nuisance algal growth around the shores. At Kezar Lake in New Hampshire compressed air has been pumped along the lake bottom in perforated plastic pipes. Bubbles released thereby have prevented the stratification of algae, thus equalizing the chemical and physical characteristics of the lake. Previous analysis of the algae had revealed a practically pure culture of the toxic *Aphanizomenon flos-acquae*. Another beautiful New Hampshire lake that grew haphazardly into a recreational center provides an example of the need for planning: industrial waste in its entering river turns its once-vivid blue waters to green when the algae bloom, and underneath is "a worrisome content of raw sewage," contributed by townspeople and summer residents, whose cottages ring the lake.[14] It is conditions such as this that the national Clean Water Act is helping to clear up, since it can provide 70 percent of the cost of a sewage system for the community. At Lake Tahoe in California, where the water is deep and clear, a mammoth sewage filtration plant has been installed at some distance from the settlement. Few lakeside communities have the sources of revenue of Tahoe, but many have taken advantage of the federal funds for proper sewage disposal to keep the ecosystem of their waters stable.

Penalties for industrial and municipal pollution under the new Federal Water Pollution Control Amendments Act (1972) are heavy: fines of $2,000 to $25,000 per diem may be imposed for each violation.[15] Eventual secondary treatment of sewage was required for all communities by this act. The "sewage doctors" have as many schemes for the best methods of treatment as the solid waste disposal and recycling experts have. Two of the popular European systems, the Pasveer oxidation ditch and the Carrousel, are being used in the United States; they are considerably less expensive than the conventional activated sludge plant and are more trouble-free. Secondary effluent is being used to spray forests and fields in some parts of the country, thus providing irrigation and fertilizer at the same time, in contrast to Tahoe's elaborate tertiary system, which uses chemicals and electrical energy to render the remaining pollutants harmless.

Realization that water quality and the recycling of waste are of one piece with intelligent planning has produced new ideas and new legislation, one of the keys to which is landscape reclamation. National discussion on the limits to growth has also spurred new ideas on land use, and a national land use policy act has been under consideration by the Congress for some time. One of the earliest applications of these ideas is contained in legislation proposed by Senator Edward Kennedy for the islands off the coast of Massachusetts, the scenic values of which are in danger from overpopulation. The Nantucket Sound Islands Trust Bill is designed to preserve the natural environment by designating land which is to remain wild, in contrast to town lands designed for certain forms of development. Summer vacation houses will be limited, as will tourism. The *New York Times* has backed the bill, which is now under discussion locally as well as in Washington.

On the continent itself, attention is once again being paid to river basins, but with an emphasis different from that of the earlier Tennessee Valley Authority or the Water Resources Commission, which has done valuable work in the west. The author of one new bill is Senator Abraham Ribicoff, who proposed in 1969 a Connecticut Historic Riverway in an attempt to prevent destruction of the cultural and physical environment of the Connecticut River Valley, which actually runs through three states. Ribicoff's emphasis is on reclamation as well as protection; in 1972 he introduced another bill dealing with the Housatonic River Basin. [16] This important river, which runs from Massachusetts into Long Island Sound, is threatened not only by pollution but by uncontrolled development as well. Pointing out that because the river flows through state lines and through many New England towns no concerted effort has ever been made to preserve it, Senator Ribicoff noted that only the federal government can serve as the catalyst to bring the diverse elements of the region together. His bill proposed a Housatonic River Valley Trust, with three classifications of land: (1) Lands forever wild, in which no development would be allowed; (2) Scenic preservation lands, in which the present density of development would not be increased; (3) Town lands, in which local governments would have the authority and responsibility for all land use decisions. "What is needed," wrote Ribicoff, "is a vehicle to channel the inevitable forces of development in such a way as to protect the cultural and natural resources without disrupting the local economy and the residents' life styles." The Trust would have members representing the state, the local towns' conservation groups, and others. A step in the proper direction was taken in 1976 when the Congress passed a new law authorizing a study by the Bureau of Recreation, which subsequently determined that forty-one miles of the Housatonic were eligible for inclusion in the National Wild and Scenic Rivers System.[17]

Interest in community appearance has spurred the growth of local conservation commissions, state and federal open space grants, subdivision regulations, litter ordinances, and other stimuli and curbs unknown a generation ago. Landscape esthetics, formerly not thought to be within the jurisdiction of the courts, received its due in the United States Supreme Court in 1964, when Justice William O. Douglas gave his now-famous opinion in the case of *Berman* v. *Parker:*

> The concept of the public welfare is broad and inclusive. . . . The values it represents are spiritual and physical, esthetic as well as monetary. It is within the power of the legislature to determine that the community should be beautiful as well as healthy, spacious as well as clean, well balanced as well as carefully patrolled.[18]

To restore and maintain the earth after all the devastation that has occurred since Marsh's day will take time, but the acknowledgement that concerted action and development reaching through the whole of society is now possible is both salutary and promising.

The leading case of scenic preservation involving historic interest also dealt with a view across a river. The estate of George Washington at Mount Vernon, on the Virginia side of the Potomac River, was the earliest and most important example of historic preservation in the United States. It was protected by purchase by the Mount Vernon Ladies Association over one hundred years ago. Nevertheless, in 1955 the magnificent view across the river was threatened by the proposal that an oil tank farm be constructed on the opposite bank. The land was bought by a public-spirited member of Congress, but immediately thereafter the local government proposed to build a sewage treatment plant next door, and further action had to be taken. In 1961 the whole area across the river was declared a national park, the land to be protected by scenic easements donated by private citizens, who were afforded tax relief by the state of Maryland, which had jurisdiction over that bank of the Potomac.[19]

This was scenic preservation on a grand scale, requiring the greatest joining together of private, foundation, and government bodies to be undertaken in the United States just for protecting beauty, or "borrowed scenery," as it is called in Japan. An example from that country is the Green Zone of Kyoto which regulates urbanization in certain areas, particularly the Kyoto Hills, where, in the Acashyama district, building is entirely prohibited and indemnification has been available to property owners since 1966. Rimmed by these hills and now protected by height regulations in the central areas, Kyoto is one of the few large metropolitan centers of the world which has retained most of its original skyline.

One can find in the less developed countries the beginnings of preservation for both the cultural and natural heritage. Wildlife refuges have been established in many nations in both Asia and Africa. Among cultural concerns have been monuments of various kinds and their surroundings. Both these concerns are defined in articles 1 and 2 of UNESCO's Convention Concerning the Protection of the World Cultural and Natural Heritage. This convention (1972) established the World Heritage Committee, which maintains a list of threatened properties and administers a fund for international financial and technical assistance.

My own experience on three UNESCO' technical assistance missions with others—to Jamaica, Prambanan and Borobudur in Indonesia, and the Kathmandu Valley in Nepal—prompts some observations. All three missions involved consideration of the infrastructure in the vicinity of historic places and national monuments.

The problems inherent in the vicinity of the magnificent monuments of Prambanan near Jogjakarta have as much to do with social adaptability as with financial feasibility. A village market should be moved, an outdoor theater relocated, and local ways of agricultural production adapted to the creation of an archaeological park encompassing the whole. Since it is anticipated that funds will be forthcoming in due course for the restoration and protection of the monuments, the problems resolve themselves into matters of access, routing of traffic, and prevention of vandalism. Thieves have been active on the archaeological sites, making

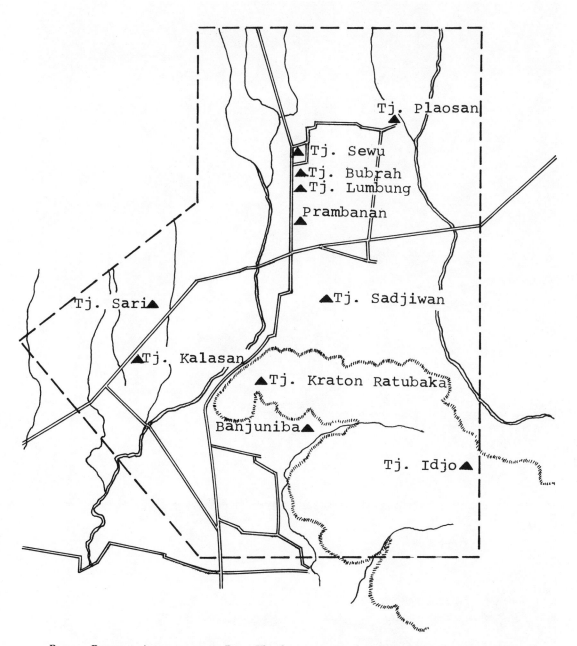

PLAN OF PROPOSED ARCHAEOLOGICAL PARK. The three main temples of Prambanan are dedicated to Siva, Brahma, and Vishnu, forming the natural center of a large neighborhood of monuments, some still hidden in the jungle. The archaeological park would be administered by the Indonesian Ministry of Education and Culture, which would control village expansion and exploitation of the area.

In the vicinity of Prambanan, where restoration is in progress, are many smaller but important monuments and temples, all in need of protection from vandals and needing proper access paths as well as other tourist facilities. Shown here is a sculptural relief from Plaosan, one of these sepulchral monuments.

necessary a system of policing and protection hitherto foreign to the easy access enjoyed by farmers and agricultural workers. The local market frustrates access by tourists and pilgrims. The outdoor theater built for productions of the Ramayana dances is located within the outer walls of the main temple complex, where it impedes site investigation; it should be moved across the river. A second village may have to give up a fringe of land and houses to a new access route if the original approach to the temples from the east is reopened.

Here it is necessary to be aware of the customs and beliefs of an agricultural population before making any changes such as those suggested above. The jurisdictions of two sultanates are involved, since the dividing line between Surakarta and Jogjakarta bisects the archaeological zone. Yet the setting up of such a zone is imperative for the future development and interpretation of the cultural property. The problem is twofold: to retain as much irrigated agricultural land as possible in a country which must import rice to feed its millions of people, and to introduce cultural tourism in the way least disruptive to agricultural pursuits and to village life. To do this, very careful planning of the road system and tourist facilities will be of prime importance, and collaboration among the agricultural department, the village authorities, and the folklorists will be necessary to ensure that the influx of city dwellers and tourists be accomplished smoothly.

At Borobudur the conditions are different and the scenery wilder. The spot is further away from Jogjakarta among rivers and mountains, but fortunately not immediately adjacent to the district's active volcano, Merapi. This very important Buddhist monument, a tremendous isolated stupa covered with stone sculpture celebrating the life of the Founder, is being restored by dismantling, cleaning, and reerecting the entire fabric. Originally earth-filled, the monument was in danger of collapse when UNESCO undertook to raise the money for this expensive operation. Among the national gifts was one of one and a half million dollars raised in the United States from private donors and corporations. Other national funds came from the Netherlands and Japan.

The comfort of pilgrims and the demands of cultural tourism require that certain elements of the infrastructure be inserted discreetly in the "natural frame" of Borobudur. Two nearby smaller religious monuments can be connected to the

BOROBUDUR FROM THE AIR. The "cosmic mountain" Borobudur (above) is one of the pilgrimage centers of world Buddhism. The mural artifacts of five galleries depict scenes from the epic of the Gautama Buddha. They are crowned by the stupas of "an upper world without form" and on another level become a massive open-air museum. Borobudur was rescued from the surrounding jungle in 1814 by Sir Stamford Raffles (present topography is pictured in aerial photo at right). Today it is being rescued from the elements by UNESCO experts (of which the author was one) who are occupied with the dismantling and restoring of the entire monument, stone by stone, as well as improving the infrastructure for the purposes of cultural tourism.

VII 1066/IV-D

main shrine by a new pilgrimage route, a river must be bridged, and a tourist center (hidden from the approaches) should be built below the monument itself. Thirty miles of the road from Jogjakarta need improvement as well as constant maintenance, because of frequent damage from the elements.[20]

This holy place, so beautiful in its present natural setting, is a pilgrimage center for the whole of Asia and the Buddhist world, which reaches it now with some difficulty. Accessibility for large numbers of people must be the established goal, but it must be achieved without overbuilding or disfiguration.

Both Indonesian examples point up the importance of preserving the natural frame of historic or religious structures and monuments. The delimitation of boundaries under agency control may vary, from a "visual corridor" to a "valley rim" to an entire watershed. In the case of the valley of Kathmandu, a UNESCO team is recommending varying degrees of protection for the entire historic valley, which not only contains many hundreds of historic temples, stupas, and chaityas but many sacred forests and of course all the rivers which play such an important part in the religious life of the Nepalese.

Scenic preservation in the Kathmandu Valley entails a major effort to maintain the Nepalese cultural identity (which takes in traditional methods of building and planning, rice terracing, and religious observance), while at the same time improving the standard of living by the introduction of modern industrial production and distribution. Natural sites in the overcrowded valley are constantly populated, mainly for purposes of recreation or religious ceremony. Even now, most people come to picnic places and viewing sites on foot, so one will not find parked cars or stations for petrol sales disfiguring the sites. Neither will one find much litter, since food containers are made of biodegradable material like leaves and straw. Well-trodden paths are everywhere and are wide enough for most uses since the conventional "beast of burden" is husband, wife, or child.

A description will indicate something of the character and importance of these paths in the daily life of the villagers. It is of the path to Matatirtha, both pilgrimage route and working thoroughfare. Nobody knows how old this stone path is, but a recent recommendation proposed that it be archaeologically investigated.

INTRUSIONS ON SCENIC AND CULTURAL VALUES. A cement factory has been erected by the sacred Bagmati River as it leaves the Chobar Gorge, famous in Nepalese mythology, thus destroying the amenities of the best-loved viewing and picnic ground in the Kathmandu Valley.

From the highway bus stop on the road to the west and India, a path through the village turns into a lane roughly paved with stones and bordered with rose hedges smothered in May bloom. At this season the wheat harvest is in progress . . . the men have wheat sheaves balanced on poles on their backs, the women carrying bundles of grain. Children, goats and chickens are everywhere. A family of ducks guzzles in the green water.

The path goes gently up the hill, following a stream, which in places flows over it. Outside the village there is an occasional Newari house with buffaloes tethered outside and wheat stacks being threshed by women. Then the grassy upland is reached, whence distant views of Kathmandu and the village of Kirtipur on its high ridge can be seen, with a backing of fantastic cloud tapestry. One passes a water mill and approaches a brick-walled enclosure built under the steep slope of a mountain of the Nagarjun range, resting for a moment under a Bodi tree near the entrance. Inside is a large space, but it is not dominated by a stupa. There is a small chaitya and a series of carved waterspouts from which the stream one has been following gushes out. It is captured in a square masonry pond (the whole vast enclosure is paved) where ritual bathing takes place. Early in May thousands of people congregate here for Matatirtha Snan; just once a year it is a pilgrimage place where people go in memory of their mothers. (There is a shrine for father-worship too, but in another place on another day.) On an ordinary evening the big courtyard is empty and silent except for the sound of rushing water . . . the source of the little river coming out of the mountain.

Walking back to the bus stop, people who work in the capital mingle with the wheat carriers on their way up the path toward home. Shod or barefoot, it is the way everyone goes in this part of the countryside.

In the matter of national traditions Nepal offers many lessons to the rest of the world. A reliance on foot traffic is one of these. It will be regrettable if the new generation forsakes the old ways of getting about in favor of the personalized vehicular mobility which has caused so many death-dealing problems elsewhere. The compactness of towns and villages, also a traditional factor in the lifestyle of the valley, is aided by the tradition of living together, so that suburbanization was a minor phenomenon until quite recently. This unusual situation has been ex-

SWAYAMBHU BUDDHIST SHRINE NEAR THE CITY OF KATHMANDU. Here the Buddha rested. It is one of the most important religious complexes in Nepal; consequently, the master plan for the Conservation of Monuments initiated by UNESCO has recommended that it be declared within a monument zone, ensuring its protection.

plained in a socioeconomic survey initiated by the Department of Housing, Building, and Physical Planning which describes the long history of urbanization in Kathmandu Valley towns. No one lives in squatter settlements or temporary housing. Unemployment among heads of households is low and family structure is highly stable. Immigration is relatively low and most inhabitants are lifelong residents, not only of one town, but of a single block and even a single house. The worst area in a town, from a physical standpoint, is usually the edge or riverside portion.

It is most important for the future of the valley to maintain and reinforce the established folk tradition of living in towns. Apart from establishing the protection and restoration of religious monuments as priorities, the UNESCO team's recommendations included creating a natural frame around important historic towns (to prevent urban sprawl); setting height and materials restrictions in the town centers (the traditional building material is brick, but new tall buildings of reinforced concrete have affected both the skyline and the immediate vicinity of religious compounds); assuring protection of viewing sites of the Himalayas, together with views of characteristic tiers of rice fields; enforcing restrictions on road-building operations; and preventing of hillside erosion, which takes the form of slash-and-burn agriculture on formerly wooded slopes.

As we have seen, each country, district, city, or town has individual scenic conservation problems which may be unique, but which often can be solved by experience gained or regulations already applied elsewhere. One simple example is the British system of tree preservation orders. It can be useful in any town or city in the world; the results will vary, but only as local administrations vary in aptitude or integrity. Another is the international concept of district conservation rather than reliance on a listing of individual buildings. There is already a comprehensive guide to the preservation of historic sites in the form of a protective inventory which covers every conceivable scenic problem in cities or countryside worldwide.[21] With a growing consciousness of scenic values, we can now influence decisively the technical and social issues which lead to the impairment of those values.

THE ALL-EMBRACING VIEW

Now that we have looked at the scenic universe in several perspectives, it is time to ask a few questions.

What is the state of the art? Although, in Constable's words, "we see nothing unless we understand," it can be said that we have advanced from the days when a landscape was nothing more than a pretty picture bathed in a sunset glow. This is in spite of, or perhaps partly because of, the fact that we live in chaotic surroundings—an environment that has deteriorated in many ways in the aftermath of the Industrial Revolution. But we know more about what we are seeing and realize that there are hidden values worth preserving and enhancing in the scene before us. How this is to be done is receiving more and more attention. A "natural features" theory of law is developing, and the "nuisance theory" is expanding to include the right of the public to enjoy unspoiled scenery. This right is slowly broadening from the protection of marshes and wetlands, formerly deemed "useless" by all except sportsmen, to river valleys, coastlands, and hilltops; this extension has been brought about in part by those who have expounded the tenets of ecology, with its emphasis on linkages, food chains, and symbiosis.

The invisible realities of landscape must be understood if public interest is to be harnessed for the drive toward enhancing esthetic values. Since everything one sees in the landscape is property, public or private, ownership may be the single most important factor to be reckoned with when the public interest is under consideration. Property can be made subject to environmental controls, but it is important to know the type of property and its potentials, as in the case of land abutting lakes or rivers, which can be developed for private residential development or public recreation, retained as farmland or left as wilderness. The choices may depend upon the state of the economy or the policy of the local government, among other factors. Hence the rising interest in land-use regulation, more advanced in the nations of northwestern Europe than elsewhere at present, but growing in North America and recognized as being especially important where ownership may be in several hands and not acquired by the public.

Can a course of action be devised which would channel the new esthetic interest in our surroundings through the appropriate social and cultural institutions toward the goal of a pleasing environment? Yes, if the goals of society are broadened to include esthetic ones. Here it is important to advance beyond the equivalent of ministries of fine arts, which in some countries have spearheaded urban and rural design improvement; we must advance too beyond the goal of a healthy, safe environment, which, important though it is, cannot be sufficient for the task. The positive goal of living in beautiful surroundings must be made an article in the defense of nations—and it must be funded. Some isolated programs come close to providing the necessary esthetic satisfactions—the planting of forests can be one of these, and so can be the regulation of mineral extraction, which unchecked can involve the destruction of a whole county and beyond. Some everyday activities which prevent esthetic contemplation are still tolerated by the public; stream channelization is one of these, and it is pursued by governments with blind persistence. Clearly, there has been no overriding esthetic policymaking on a national scale, but it is encouraging that some economists have begun to examine values formerly considered too vague to quantify. If a cost figure can be put against esthetic experience, wilderness, which is becoming scarcer, should rate highly. Societies can work out the amounts they are willing to pay for it. Some schemes already include esthetic factors; one, for wild rivers, treats items like the view of a valley from above, the view from below, the flood plain vista, and the appearance of the channel.[1] Although these factors are not rated as highly as water quality and habitat for living species, the fact that they are included at all is a step in the right direction and a signal to departments of the environment that there are other values to be considered besides the purely physical. It is salutary to discover that beauty can be priced. As the ancient Chinese proverb goes, "If thou hast two cakes of bread, sell one and buy thyself lilies."

Can city and regional planning help to ensure scenic values? If it is the right kind of planning it is more than desirable. Most people can remember the planning policies of governments after the second world war which produced superhighway programs, neighborhood demolition, "high-rise" housing, and other supposed "benefits" to society. This phase is now drawing to a close in many of the developed nations, but in the least developed parts of the world Western planning policies of the fifties and sixties are still being emulated. Ancient cities are being surrounded by ring-roads without thought to their effect on the city's heart, hotels are being built on unspoilt cliffs and beaches in defiance of the principles of cultural tourism, and jungles are being denuded of trees to accommodate resettlement projects. It is useless to point out that these are not planning activities at all, that they are the reverse: they have the blessing of governmental and international agencies and are considered important elements of the infrastructure. A high government official's pet project in a low-profiled historic Asian city, admired throughout the world, is to adorn it with a revolving restaurant on a two-hundred foot tower "like the ones in Rotterdam and Frankfurt."

Unfortunately, the fascination with modern technology is worldwide, and although we should not wish to deny "progress" to those less fortunate than ourselves, progress can get out of hand very easily. There is a danger inherent in the current preoccupation with technique, not only for the planners of technique, but for other segments of society as well. Fascination with technology is born of very human desires for material diversity, as well as for weaponry, space exploration, and mechanical gadgetry of dubious value. Belated realization that the cost in environmental and moral damage has been extensive has encouraged new approaches—facet planning, for instance, which deals with single-function social activities, such as the revival of metropolitan mass transportation, land trusts and land banks, steady state economic plans, and others. Forward motion, as George Steiner puts it, is being replaced as an ideal by cultural circularity. The inability of populations to solve the problem of exponential growth (a characteristic of societies as well as of bank interest and capital investment) so far has prevented much hope of equilibrium in an essentially finite global system. It is no wonder that planners have had to reassess their goals in the light of shifting world opinion, but it is at the same time important to be using the right tools. The demand for the synthetic function of planning is often obscured in the advocacy process or reduced to a series of small, substantive steps. But the need for a comprehensive physical plan at all levels exists. It is as foolish to attempt a national urban growth policy without one as it would be to set out to build a new town, where the need is obvious, without one. Not only is a plan needed in land-use relationships, but, as the best examples of the past demonstrate, a strong esthetic component is needed too. The new view of planning is born of the constraints imposed by ecology and conservation, together with the liberation afforded by the adoption of coherent social policies based on the gross national happiness as well as the gross national product.

Who benefits from scenic preservation and development? Since international resolutions have demanded that the national cultural and scenic patrimony be available to all people everywhere, perhaps the question is superfluous. However, there remains the problem of access, which is not yet solved by technology (public buses instead of private cars in Yosemite) or by any other means of assuaging people's hunger for the outdoors. Various suggestions like that of increasing the number of state parks, in order to lure people away from the more spectacular national and forest parks, have not proved tenable either. But egalitarian societies cannot fail in their task to make cultural attractions available to all. Problems abound in all countries, but especially in heavily populated ones. Malcolm MacEwen[2] points out that in Britain the national parks are not national, in the sense of being nationally owned, nor parks, in the sense of being freely opened to the public as of right. He suggests that they can more accurately be described as "rural conservation areas." Farmers, county councils, forestry boards, as well as the Commission on the Countryside—all have their fingers in the pie and after twenty-five years are just beginning to exercise some responsibility for cultural tourism. The gentle British landscape, man-modified for centuries, like the highly cultivated plains and valleys of the Île de France, must be considered as scenically important as the wildest goatpaths of the Pyrenees or the Abruzzi. All that one can say now is that further understanding by the public may induce respect for scenic values, thus leading to demands for action. This leads to the next question.

How can people best absorb scenic values? Principally by studying the process of landscape development together with the images of it that have been formed by the hand of the artist. The scientific methods of physical geography are important, but any other rigorous scientific approach to nature can be helpful. A most enlightening course was once given by F. J. Chittenden at Wisley; he called it

YOSEMITE VALLEY, by the painter of the American west, Albert B. Bierstadt, who made studies for the picture on a visit in 1863.

simply "Observation" and asked his students to identify and explain the processes of organic nature by the use of "found" objects in the classroom. When asked to identify the position of the cambium layer in a section of timber the class would produce as many variations as if they were playing pin the tail on the donkey. The exercise proved that the placement of the pin had to be exact. None ever forgot the importance of that fact or the need to see clearly what nature was about.

Looking to the horizon will take one far beyond the classroom—that is of course what the artist is able to do, although obviously what he perceives has varied according to the age he lived in and his own technical skills. It is the very multiplicity of images in art which is most compelling, although often confusing at first. Taste will develop, for taste is knowledge and not to be mistaken for fashion. Looking at visual images should not only be practiced but practiced hard; the same can be said for developing architectural judgment by studying townscape. Amateurism is not to be discounted here, although the history of art and architecture can provide a useful background if it is not indulged in purely for pedagogical expertise. There is no substitute for firsthand observation—going out into the country and into the city streets to observe what is seen with one's accumulated knowledge of literature and art. Each situation has its esthetic statement to make, negative or positive, and we are fortunate that standards have been set up in times other than our own. No matter that amateurs like Price and Knight have quarreled over the meaning of the picturesque or the beautiful; we know that beauty exists because man has always admired beautiful things. Although each person will see a landscape somewhat differently, if his opinion is informed it will help to communicate the scene to others who have not the time or the inclination to live up to the demands of the past. All elements of society must come eventually to realize that scenic values are an essential part of the cultural life of nations, that their desecration is a crime against the people, and that they can be cherished and enhanced only by the development of esthetic judgment. Further, it must be realized that this kind of judgment can be applied to all the arts and sciences, for, as the philosophers tell us, the ultimate satisfactions are esthetic ones.

Among the most important of human rights is the right to see beautiful things wherever one may find oneself. The circle is narrowing in an alarming way. Privacy is expensive—and, in any case, who can be content with admiring his own rosebush or some other personal possession when it has to be screened off as much as possible from surroundings that are unsightly?

Finally, having formed some opinions on scenic values, what can we do to capture them for posterity? Basic issues here are political. Man, records the Duc de Levis Mirepoix, is a social animal who must live with his fellow creatures. As an independent animal, he is forced to face up to them or avoid them. But society only exists by grace of the interdependence of its members. What is it that produces any kind of agreement? La Politesse![3] The economist Mansholt adds, "I have plenty of sympathy for a life à la Robinson Crusoe but I don't believe it is possible for more than three hundred million human beings,"[4] a number which the world long ago exceeded. So we are forced to cooperate somehow. But we are still in an age of confrontation and avoidance, in terms of the environment. Some of us want to build up while others want to tear down, the latter often being secretive about their plans. The stream alongside which we have a picnic, whether it is in China or the Bronx, should be pure. So should the air. These are the externalities of landscape viewing, and some countries have progressed beyond the stage of merely analyzing the effects of impurities in the air and water, which have ranged from destroying the sculptures on Venetian churches to killing the inhabitants of a Japanese village. Economic issues are involved here, with the possibilities of manipulation of nature by society far exceeding what was thought to be necessary in the departed days of laissez-faire. It is thus absurd to think any longer of the natural versus the man-made in terms of environmental values, any more than it is necessary to think of antagonism between the past and the present, which ideally should merge in the consciousness of man. Man must take on the role of custodian of nature and of the past; he is the sole animal who understands the contributions of civilizations other than his own, contributions psychologically important to his own welfare. Coexistence has become a vital concern of present-day society—coexistence with nature and the rest of the cultural patrimony contained in the past. A symbol of this is the setting up of a secretariat of the environment by the United Nations in Nairobi, demonstrating not only the willingness of the UN to tackle third-world problems, but also the readiness of developing countries to make environmental problems a subject of major importance.

A beginning has been made to bridge a gap wider than the Gorge of Tempe—the yawning chasm between the unbridled exploitation of technology on the one side and full development of the cultural patrimony on the other. The gap will only be bridged when the esthetic values of society are properly understood.

NOTES

Landscape and Science

1 Among the eighteenth-century philosophers whose works provided food for discussion of natural beauty were Francis Hutcheson, David Hume, and Edmund Burke.

2 John Ruskin, *Praeterita* (London, 1949), p. 309.

3 Ibid., p. 414.

4 William T. Stearn, "Linnean Classification, Nomenclature and Method," appendix in Wilfred Blunt, *The Compleat Naturalist* (New York, 1971), p. 245.

5 "The planting of pineta originated in the beginning of the present century." (John Gould Vietch, *Coniferae*, London, 1881, p. 321.) David Douglas, the Scottish botanist, was a prime introducer of these trees from western North America; in Britain the names of Westonbirt, Bodnant, and Sheffield Park mark their new homes. Successive dukes of Atholl in Perthshire, planted between 1730 and 1826 fourteen million trees covering ten thousand acres. The Hunnewell estate at Wellesley, Massachusetts, planted in 1851 and still in the same family, has splendid specimens of coniferous trees, as well as an Italian garden overlooking a body of water which "quite leads us to suppose we are on the lake at Como." (Henry Winthrop Sargent, "A Supplement," in his enlarged edition of A. J. Downing, A *Treatise on the Theory and Practice of Landscape Gardening* [New York, 1859], p. 444).

6 In the Americas the earliest botanical collection may have been the pre-Aztec gardens of Tetzcutzinco, thirty miles northeast of Mexico City, which were brought to perfection in the mid-fifteenth century and thus antedate Padua by a century. For illustrations of the archaeological excavations there see *Country Life*, June 12, 1975, pp. 1570–71.

7 Alan Eyre, *The Botanic Gardens of Jamaica* (London, 1966).

8 For a description of the house, the seed house, and what was in the collection see Emily Reed Cheston, *John Bartram, 1699–1777* (Philadelphia, 1953).

9 For a biography of the founder see Alan Gross, *Charles Joseph La Trobe* (Melbourne, 1956).

10 Anthony Trollope, *Australia*, ed. P. D. Edwards and R. B. Joyce (St. Lucia, 1967), pp. 643–44.

11 Crosbie Morrison, M.Sc., *Melbourne's Garden* (Melbourne, 1957), p. 28.

12 S. H. Hutner, "Botanical Gardens and Horizons in Algal Research" in P. Dansereau, ed., *Challenge for Survival* (New York and London, 1970), p. 209.

13 "The phase microscope, pre-mixed color media, synthetic sea salts, screw-cap culture tubes, small efficient centrifuges, mail-order pressure cookers and cheap fluorescent lighting make it possible even for apartment dwellers to take up the study of creatures of pond and ocean." Ibid., p. 215.

14 S. M. Walters, "The Role of Botanic Gardens in Conservation," *Journal of the Royal Horticultural Society* 98 (July 1973): 311–15.

15 Jacques Ellul, *The Technological Society*, trans. J. Wilkinson (New York, 1964). Ellul, French sociologist, Catholic layman, and a former leader of the Resistance, published *La Technique* in 1954. On the advice of Aldous Huxley it was translated into English in 1964. It details how society has been technicized,

rendered efficient, and diminished in the process. A difficult book, it has nevertheless had a strong appeal to my students at Yale. Robert Theobald, writing in *The Nation*, called it one of the most important books of the second half of the twentieth century. Ellul has been compared with Mumford, Spengler, Veblen, and others, but his own contribution is substantial.

16   Ibid., p. 27.
17   George Perkins Marsh, *Man and Nature: Physical Geography as Modified by Human Action*, ed. D. Lowenthal (Cambridge, Mass., 1965), p. 268. (The work was originally published in 1864.)
18   Ibid., p. 279.
19   *New York Times*, Dec. 16, 1971.
20   A change comparable to that which took place when men began to enjoy mountain scenery. Until Rousseau used mountains to illustrate his doctrine "what is savage is noble, what is civilized, corrupt" and de Saussure became the creator of scientific alpinism, breaking ground for Wordsworth's naturalistic descriptions of the Westmoreland fells, mountains were universally regarded as demonic. Even Chateaubriand described them as "ugly lumps." (Early dissenters from this view were Dante, Petrarch, and Leonardo da Vinci, who made a scientific investigation of a glacier.)
21   Lynton K. Caldwell, "Centers of Excellence for the Study of Human Ecology," in *Proceedings of Symposium of Human Ecology*, U.S. Department of Health, Education and Welfare (Washington, D.C., 1968), pp. 58 ff.
22   H. G. Wells, *Anticipations of the Reaction of Mechanical and Scientific Progress upon Human Life and Thought* (New York and London, 1902), p. 68.
23   Odell Shephard, *The Harvest of a Quiet Eye* (Boston, 1927), p. 83.
24   Bernard Berenson, *Seeing and Knowing* (New York, 1953), p. 7.
25   M. D. Vernon, "Seeing What We Want To See," *Times Literary Supplement*, Oct. 25, 1974, p. 1193.
26   Richard L. Gregory, "How We See and Hear Things," *Journal of the Royal Society of Arts* (August 1972): 630 ff.
27   M. Minnaert, *Light and Color in the Open Air* (New York, 1954), p. 132.
28   M. W. Beresford, *Time and Place: An Inaugural Lecture* (Leeds, 1961).
29   Harold Carter, *The Study of Urban Geography* (London, 1972), pp. 1 f.
30   V. Ivanov, "Monuments and Society," in *Symposium on Monuments and Society* (Paris, 1971), p. 18.
31   A. Geikie, *Landscape in History and Other Essays* (London, 1905), pp. 25 ff.

Landscape and Art

1   *Oxford English Dictionary*, s.v. "landscape": 1603, Sylvester, *Du Bartas* 1, vii. 13.
2   *Oxford Companion to Art*, "Roman Art," p. 999.
3   Sherman E. Lee, *Chinese Landscape Painting*, rev. ed. (New York, n.d.), p. 18.
4   "Chinese Once More Giving Foreigners Chance to See Kweilin Scenery that Inspired Ancient Artists," *New York Times*, July 27, 1973, p. 5.
5   Max J. Friedlander, *Landscape-Portrait-Still Life: Their Origin and Development* (New York, 1965), p. 21.
6   Ibid., p. 73
7   *Oxford Companion to Art*, "Perspective," p. 861.
8   Joan Gadol, *Leon Battista Alberti* (Chicago and London, 1969), p. 198.

9   Kenneth Clark, *Landscape Into Art* (London, 1949), p. 19. There is also a Dürer aquarelle of a small fortified town in the Val d'Arco in the Louvre, 18597 (A144).

10 Gadol, *Alberti*, p. 132.

11 Until much later, when French painters made a fetish of it. "Courbet had joined the group and inevitably influenced the younger men; yet he in return was affected by their refusal not merely to accept studio lighting, the picture lit as if by a hole in the top of a cave. Nor were they content, as Corot and Millet had been, to choose effects of twilight or grey skies. They wanted full sunlight, light everywhere, *la peinture claire*." Stephen Gwynn, *Claude Monet and His Garden* (London, 1934), p. 25.

12 In the United States, where portraiture and historical painting maintained preeminence after the Revolution, the Hudson River School became the first body of painters to celebrate landscape for its own sake. The mode was Romantic, and at least some of the artists had painted in Europe. See Christopher Tunnard, "Reflections on the Course of Empire and other Architectural Fantasies of Thomas Cole, N.A.," *The Architectural Review*, vol. 104, pp. 291–94.

13 Wordsworth admits that he is putting the best face on the Lake District that he possibly can, but in spite of his evocation of the Simplon in verse, his remarks on Italian scenery will surprise the reader of the *Guide*. Wordsworth's Lake District has marvelous cloud effects compared with "the cerulean vacancy of Italy," a country which has chestnut and walnut trees "growing to a considerable height," but even their foliage "is not equal in beauty to the natural product of this climate." The vine makes a dull, formal appearance in the landscape and Wordsworth wishes that the splendid promontory of Bellagio were clothed with "the natural variety of one of our parks." E. de Selincourt, ed., *Wordsworth's Guide to the Lakes*, fifth ed. 1835 (London, 1970), pp. 46 ff.

14 The garden at Rydal Mount, where tourists can now stay, is reputed to have been laid out by the poet. He was no devotee of the fashion for the picturesque, which he called "a strong infection of the age . . ./Bent overmuch on superficial things . . . with meagre novelties/Of colour and proportion" (*The Prelude*, book 12).

15 From Ruskin's preface to Somervell's "Protest Against the Extension of the Railways in the Lake District," 1877. A similar problem exists today. As this is written, protests focus on a projected highway to run from Whitehaven, on the coast, right through the northern part of the District. Of the day visitors from home who visit the Keswick-Borrowdale area, 57 percent come by car, 30 percent by bus or motorcoach, and only 7 percent by train. See Roy Millward and Adrian Robinson, *The Lake District* (London, 1970), p. 260.

16 Vernon Lee, "The Lie of the Land," *Limbo and Other Essays* (London, 1897), p. 45.

17 Albert Boime, *The Academy and French Painting in the Nineteenth Century* (London and New York, 1971), pp. 133–47.

18 Ibid., p. 140.

19 John Piper, *Buildings and Prospects* (London, 1948), p. 8.

20 Balzac's assessment of James Fenimore Cooper's novels, in *Lettres sur la Litterature*.

21 Samuel Rogers, *Balzac and the Novel* (Madison, Wis., 1953), p. 49. Flaubert was not lacking in visual appreciation of landscapes. "The palm . . . an architectural tree. Everything in Egypt seems made for architecture . . . the planes of the fields, the vegetation, the human anatomy, the horizon lines." Francis Steegmuller, *Flaubert in Egypt* (Boston, 1973), p. 58, translated from the "Travel Notes and Letters."

22 *Hard Times*, chap. 5.

23 *The Wings of the Dove* (New York, 1946), chap. 32, p. 320.

24 *The American Scene* (New York, 1967), p. 335.

25 W. D. Howells's utopian novels are *A Traveler from Altruria* and *Through the Eye of the Needle*.

26 Upton Sinclair, *The Metropolis* (New York, 1908), p. 180.

27 Lynes makes this point in a speech, "The Writer and the City," at the Yale Civic Art Conference in 1952.

28 Thomas Kennerly Wolfe's descriptive pieces are to be found in his volumes *The Electric Kool-Aid Acid Test* and *The Pump House Gang*, both 1968.

29 *On the Road* (New York, 1959), p. 141.

30 *Country Life*, Nov. 27, 1975, p. 1457.

The Garden

1 Pliny, *Letters and Panegyricus*, trans. B. Radice. Loeb Classical Library edition, book 1, letter 9.

2 Ibid., letter 3.

3 *De Re Aedificatori*, book 9, chap. 4.

4 Georgina Masson, "Italian Flower Collectors' Gardens in Seventeenth Century Italy," in *The Italian Garden*, ed. David R. Coffin (Washington, D.C., 1972).

5 J. C. Shepherd and Geoffrey Jellicoe, *Gardens and Design* (London and New York, 1927), p. 127.

6 See, among others, Christopher Hussey, *English Gardens and Landscapes* (London, 1967), and David Green, *Gardener to Queen Anne* (1956).

7 Hussey, *English Gardens*, p. 38.

8 *Five Miscellaneous Essays by Sir William Temple*, ed. S. H. Monk (Ann Arbor, 1963), pp. 29–30.

9 "A Note on Sharawadgi," *Modern Language Notes* (1930): 221.

10 Hugh Honour, *Chinoiserie: The Vision of Cathay*, Icon Edition (New York, 1973; first published in 1961). See part 6, "The Anglo-Chinese Garden," pp. 143 ff.

11 Basil Gray, "Lord Burlington and Father Ripa's Chinese Engravings," *British Museum Quarterly* 22 (1960): 40–43.

12 Father Matteo Ripa (1682–1746), an Italian missionary priest, was attached to the Chinese court from 1711 to 1723. In 1724 he visited London and was entertained at the Court of St. James. In 1703 the Emperor K'ang-hsi had commenced building a series of palaces in South Manchuria, about one hundred and fifty miles northeast of Peking, and ordered thirty-six views of them painted to illustrate his own poems. With some difficulty, owing to his lack of expertise and equipment, these were engraved by the priest.

13 Rudolf Wittkower, "English Neo-Palladianism, the Landscape Garden, China, and the Enlightenment," *L'Arte*, no. 6 (1969): 40.

14 Georgina Masson, *Italian Gardens* (London, 1961), p. 36.

15 Ibid., p. 269.

16 Honour, *Chinoiserie*, p. 143.

17 There is not much evidence of the Chinese taste in gardens in North America, although handsome rooms such as the well-known one at Gunston Hall still exist. There is a Chinese Chippendale railing at Jefferson's Monticello, and a Chinese pavilion, adorned with philosophical mottoes, at "Belfield," the painter Charles Willson Peale's *ferme ornée* outside Philadelphia. Osvald Sirén mentions a garden in

Louisiana, which I have not seen. Several eighteenth-century garden houses seem to have the roof lines of their Chinese counterparts, but without the decoration. The gazebo in the garden of the Shaw mansion in New London, Connecticut, is a case in point.

Curiously, a reconstruction of the "Chinese" part of William Paca's garden at Annapolis is now being completed: Paca's magnificent house has been preserved and the garden restored by Historic Annapolis, Inc. Peale wrote that he painted Paca (governor of Maryland and signer of the Declaration of Independence) in his garden; the portrait shows an irregular pond and a Chinese bridge. These have now been recreated on the evidence of the painting, the site of the bridge having been discovered by archaeological evidence after the demolition of a two-hundred-room hotel. The architect Orin Bullock designed the present bridge. As the president of Historic Annapolis writes, it is difficult to believe that such an enterprise would succeed in twentieth-century America, but she believes that the garden project was given a great impetus by the 1966 President's Conference on Natural Beauty. I am indebted to Mrs. J. M. P. Wright of the above-mentioned preservation society and to John N. Pearce, historic preservation officer of the Maryland Historical Trust, which owns the garden, for this information and illustrations.

18 He advised his readers that it was hard to tell, in a Brownian garden, whether one was walking in a pleasure ground or in a common meadow.

19 Mason went further, attributing the landscape garden to the spirit of "LIBERTY" (that great principle of the Enlightenment) extending itself "to the very fancies of individuals."

20 Mavis Batey, "Oliver Goldsmith: An Indictment of Landscape Gardening," in *Furor Hortensis*, ed. Peter Willis (Edinburgh, 1974), p. 59.

21 A tributary of the Nonette, that important little river which provides the main attraction for some of the loveliest chateau gardens of the Ile de France (Ermenonville, as well as Versigny, Chablis, the Abbaye de la Victoire, and Lenôtre's Chantilly), gliding through ornamental canals and over artificial cascades, before it finally joins the Oise.

22 For an account of the work of Ramée see Christopher Tunnard, "Joseph-Jacques Ramée: Architect of Union College," *Union Worthies*, no. 19 (Schenectady, N.Y. 1964).

23 Edward Malins, *English Landscaping and Literature* (London, 1966), p. 11.

24 *Tour in England, Ireland and France in the Years 1826–29 by a German Prince* (Philadelphia, 1833), p. 84. The reason for Pückler-Muskau's stay in England is not to be found in these pages.

25 Henry Wise's plan for the park at Blenheim can be seen in Hussey, *English Gardens*, plate 13.

26 *Letters and Memoirs of the Prince de Ligne*, trans. with notes by Leigh Ashton (London, 1927), p. 7.

27 Ibid., p. 180.

28 Derek Clifford, *A History of Garden Design* (New York, 1963), p. 159.

29 *Letters and Memoirs of the Prince de Ligne*, p. 96.

30 *Lectures on Landscape Gardening in Australia by the late Mr. Thomas Shepherd, of the Darling Nursery* (Sydney, 1836).

31 Hans Sedlmayr, *Art in Crisis*, trans. Brian Battershaw (London, 1957), pp. 14–20.

32 Kenneth Lemmon, *The Golden Age of Plant Hunters* (London, 1968), p. 15.

33 *Landscape Gardening and the Picturesque*, with a preface by Paul Breman (London, n.d.), item 80.

34 As quoted in Tunnard, *Gardens in the Modern Landscape* (London, 1938), p. 56.

35 Francis Jekyll, *Gertrude Jekyll: A Memoir*, with a foreword by Sir Edwin Lutyens (Northampton, Mass., n.d.), p. 168.

36 W. Robinson, F.L.S., *Garden Design and Architects' Gardens* (London, 1892), p. 38.

37 Jekyll, *Gertrude Jekyll*, p. 170.
38 Louis Aragon, *Le Paysan de Paris* (Paris, 1926), p. 147.
39 Ibid., p. 149.
40 Ibid., p. 181.
41 J. C. Krafft, *Plans des beaux jardins pittoresque de France* (Paris, 1809); *Receuil d'architecture civile* (Paris, 1812). See Osvald Sirén, *China and the Gardens of Europe* (New York, 1950), for a Krafft bibliography.
42 Tunnard, *Gardens in the Modern Landscape*. See pp. 62–68.

Townscape

1 Bernard Berenson, *Seeing and Knowing* (New York, 1953), p. 4.
2 Max Nicholson, *The Environmental Revolution* (New York, 1970), p. 118.
3 Ibid., p. 65.
4 J. W. N. Sullivan, *The Limitations of Science* (New York, 1949), p. 188.
5 *Highway as Environment*, Department of City Planning, Yale University Highway Research Project (New Haven, Conn., 1971), p. 5.
6 "There has always been something preternatural about paths . . . for not only poetry but folklore abounds with symbolic stories about them: paths that divide and become two paths, paths that lead to a golden kingdom . . . paths that not merely divide but become the twenty-one paths that lead back to Eden." Malcolm Lowry, *Hear us O Lord from Heaven Thy Dwelling-Place* (London, 1969), p. 272.
7 Derek Hudson, "English Switzerland in Surrey," *Country Life*, May 10, 1973, p. 1310.
8 R. N. Haber, "How We Remember What We See," *Scientific American* (May 1970), pp. 104 ff.
9 E. H. Gombrich, "The Visual Image," *Scientific American* (Sept. 1972).
10 Edward Malins, *English Landscaping and Literature* (London, 1966), pp. 145–47.
11 Aristotle, *Politics*, ed. Benjamin Jowett (Oxford, 1921), 1.2. 1253a.
12 Ibid., 1.2. 1252b.
13 See Mark M. Weintraub, "Ecology in an Age of Revolution," *Planning Outlook* 6, no. 1 (1970).
14 Priscilla Metcalf, "Viewpoint," *Times Literary Supplement*, Feb. 9, 1973, p. 150.
15 See *London Replanned*, by Royal Academy of Arts (London, 1942), and *Royal Academy London Plan*; extracts from the interim report.
16 Patrick Cormack, "Protecting the Skyline," *Country Life*, April 28, 1977, p. 1084.
17 Beverley Nichols, *Twenty-Five* (London, 1937), pp. 174–76.
18 Paul Schultze-Naumburg, *Kulturarbeiten: Die Gestaltung der Landschaft durch den Menschen* (Munich, 1916).
19 The reasons for the cutting were given as: the danger to pedestrians in storms, insects and butterflies breeding in them, and even the idea that poplars are ugly.
20 Camillo Sitte (1843–1903) was an early exponent of modern city planning and design. Schultze-Naumburg incorporated Sittesque principles in his use of photographs, showing lines of sight in streets and squares, but unlike Sitte he extended his explorations into the countryside.
21 Jay Appleton, *The Experience of Landscape* (New York, 1975).
22 From *Recommendations Concerning the Preservation of Cultural Property Endangered by Public or Private Works* (Paris, 1968).

23 Arts Council of Great Britain, *The Age of Neo-Classicism*; See "Neo-Classical Town Planning," by Alistair Rowan, pp. 656–60 (London, 1972).

24 Commemorating Admiral (later Baron) Rodney's victory over the French at the Battle of the Saints in 1782.

25 Nancy Mitford, as quoted by Harold Acton in *Nancy Mitford: A Memoir* (New York, 1975), p. 209.

26 See Christopher Tunnard, "The United States: Federal Funds for Rescue," in *The Conservation of Cities* (Paris, 1975).

27 Anthony Sutcliffe, *The Autumn of Central Paris* (Montreal, 1971), p. 299.

28 Francois Sorlin, "Europe: The Comprehensive Effort," in *The Conservation of Cities*, p. 73.

Landscape and Scenic Preservation

1   John Ise, *Our National Park Policy* (Baltimore, 1961), p. 13.

2   "The Worm and the Saw," *Not Man Apart*, vol. 5, no. 24 (San Francisco, 1975).

3   The "avant-projet" for this federal law embraces controls over installations of power plants, highways, public buildings, military barracks, and federal railways, as well as the protection of wild flowers and animals.

4   State of Vermont, Act 250.

5   Wilhelm Knabe, "Observations on World Wide Efforts to Reclaim Industrial Waste Land," in *Ecology and the Industrial Society*, ed. G. T. Goodman (New York, 1965), p. 263.

6   B. A. Franklin, "The Coal Rush is On," *The Strip Mining of America* (Sierra Club, 1971).

7   Walter M. Whitehill, "The Right of Cities to be Beautiful," in *With Heritage So Rich*, ed. Rains and Henderson (New York, 1966), p. 50.

8   "How Trash, Garbage, etc.," *National Observer*, Jan. 1, 1972.

9   White House Conference on Natural Beauty, *Beauty for America* (proceedings) (Washington, D.C., 1965), p. 321.

10 Ibid., pp. 154–58.

11 Mel Scott, *American City Planning Since 1890* (Berkeley, Cal., 1969), p. 32.

12 Lake Erie Congress, Great Lakes Research Institute et al., September 1971.

13 When substantial quantities of a limiting nutrient are added to a body of water, certain species of algae are favored, multiplying so fast that mats of green slime form on the surface. Finally, lacking nutrients or light, they will die and decompose, using up oxygen. Accumulation of sunken mats gradually causes the lake to fill in. See D. K. Hobson, *Detergents* (Bulletin of the Greater Victoria Environmental Center [July 1973]).

14 Hugh Moffett, "Troubles at Lake Mascoma," *Smithsonian* (May 1973), p. 70.

15 P.L. 92-500. 86 Stat. 816 (S.2770, passed into law October 18, 1972).

16 U.S., Congress, Senate, *Congressional Record*, 92nd Cong., 2d sess., 1972.

17 P.L. 94-486.

18 348 United States 26 (1954).

19 See *Beauty for America*, remarks of Representative Bolton, pp. 164–66.

20 John Pollacco and Christopher Tunnard, *Indonesia, Final Report: Cultural Tourism in Central Java* (Paris, n.d.).

21 Council of Europe, Council for Cultural Cooperation, *Protective Inventory: Criteria and Methods* (Strasbourg, n.d.).

The All-Embracing View

1   I. L. Whitman, *Uses of Small Urban River Valleys*, Baltimore: District Corps of Engineers (April 1968). Water Resources Engineers, Inc., *Fifth Progress Report: Developing Methods for Valuing Wild Rivers*, U.S. Department of the Interior (Washington, D.C., 1970).
2   Malcolm MacEwen, "Future of the National Parks," *Country Life*, July 8, 1976.
3   Le Duc de Levis Mirepoix, "Physiologie de la Politesse," *La Politesse* (Paris, 1969).
4   "Ecologie et Revolution," *Le Nouvel Observateur*, no. 397 (1972).

INDEX OF NAMES